PAT BROWN, MBA

Financial Literacy For Attorneys

"What Every Attorney Needs to Know About Money but Was Never Taught in Law School"

ABRAM 47 BROWN

First published by AbramBrown47 2025

First edition

ISBN: 978-1-967737-09-3

This book was professionally typeset on Reedsy.
Find out more at reedsy.com

Contents

Preface

Let me start by saying this: I didn't write this book to impress you with my financial credentials. I wrote this book because I've seen too many attorneys—bright, driven, highly educated professionals—struggle silently with money. And I believe it's time for that to change.

This book is part of a larger movement I've committed myself to—creating accessible, clear, and actionable financial literacy resources for professionals in high-performance, high-pressure careers. I've written financial literacy books for doctors, college coaches, and student-athletes. Now, it's time to focus on attorneys.

I've spent over two decades in financial planning, insurance, and retirement advising. I've worked with professionals from all walks of life—surgeons, entrepreneurs, professors, athletes, and yes, attorneys. And let me tell you: for all the training that law school provides, personal finance isn't part of the curriculum. That's not a knock on the legal field—it's a truth that applies to most elite professions. The problem is, when money isn't taught, it's learned the hard way. Through missed opportunities. Through stress. Through avoidable mistakes.

The legal field attracts people who are intelligent, competitive, and often deeply mission-driven. You've spent years building your expertise, growing your reputation, and climbing through a highly specialized and demanding profession. Whether you're an associate working 80-hour weeks, a solo practitioner running your own firm, or a partner juggling high-net-worth clients, chances are your personal financial strategy has taken a backseat to your legal career.

I get it. Law is consuming. But here's the catch: **you can't afford not to pay attention to your money.**

Here's what I've seen too often:

- Brilliant attorneys making six-figure incomes but living paycheck to paycheck.
- Solo practitioners with no retirement plan in place, unsure if they'll ever stop working.
- Partners with major assets but no estate plan or asset protection strategy.
- Younger lawyers burdened with student loans, credit card debt, and uncertainty.
- Successful attorneys who are secretly overwhelmed by tax complexity and irregular income.
- Professionals whose financial lives are entirely dependent on their earning ability—with no backup.

This book is for all of you.

It doesn't matter if you're just starting your legal career or approaching retirement. It doesn't matter if you're a criminal defense lawyer, a family law specialist, a tax attorney, or a managing partner at a firm. If you've ever felt uncertain, behind, or confused when it comes to your financial life—this book is here to help you take back control.

Now, let me be upfront about something: I'm not an attorney. I didn't go to law school. I don't bill by the hour. But I do know what it's like to be immersed in a career that consumes your time and mental energy. And I've made it my mission to teach people how to **make money work for them—no matter their field.**

What I've also learned over the years is that financial literacy has nothing to do with intelligence. Most of my attorney clients are among the smartest people I know. But financial decision-making is its own domain—with its own rules, tools, and traps. That's why lawyers, like anyone else, need a framework—a system for managing, growing, protecting, and ultimately transferring their wealth.

In writing this book, I took into account the specific pressures attorneys face:

- The impact of delayed earnings due to extended education and bar prep
- The often unpredictable income of solo practitioners and contingency-based work
- The golden handcuffs of BigLaw, where burnout can sabotage even high salaries
- The complexity of balancing billable hours, business development, and personal finance
- The financial risks that come with professional liability, client disputes, and firm partnerships
- The challenges of structuring retirement, estate, and tax planning in high-income brackets

This isn't a theory book. This is a playbook.

You won't find abstract concepts with no real-world application. You'll find step-by-step chapters that walk you through budgeting, student loan repayment, investing, tax strategies, retirement planning, insurance, estate planning, practice ownership, career transitions, and more. I'll also include real-life case studies and questions you can ask your CPA, financial advisor, or legal partner to get clarity and direction.

I've structured the book to match the different stages of an attorney's career:

- Law school and early career years (learning to manage debt and build a financial foundation)
- Mid-career growth (handling increasing income, taxes, and life changes)
- Business ownership or partnership (managing firm finances, compensation, and retirement plans)
- Pre-retirement and exit planning (transferring wealth, succession, legacy planning)

If you're a financial pro reading this and you serve attorneys—great. But this book was written primarily for the **attorney who knows their financial life matters, but hasn't had the time to focus on it**. I wrote it to make sure that when you leave the courtroom or step out of a client meeting, you're not left vulnerable on your own balance sheet.

And finally—this book is personal for me. I've had attorneys in my family. I've seen how hard you work, how much pressure you carry, and how often that pressure is worn as a badge of honor. But I also believe that **success shouldn't come at the cost of financial stress**. You can thrive in your career *and* have peace with your money. But it takes intention. It takes awareness. And it takes a plan.

I'm honored to be part of that journey with you.

Let's get to work.

Why Attorneys Need a Financial Literacy Guide

The Case for Clarity in the Profession of Precision

Attorneys are trained to think analytically, dissect complex issues, argue persuasively, and navigate high-stakes situations. You can interpret intricate contracts, negotiate terms in your sleep, and deliver closing arguments that shift the trajectory of a case. But when it comes to managing your own money, your legal education might have left you unprepared. And that's not your fault—it's the system's.

There's an unspoken assumption that if you're a high-functioning, highly educated professional, you'll just "figure it out." But financial literacy isn't common sense—it's a learned skillset. One that's often overlooked in law school, under-emphasized in early career mentorship, and put on the back burner until it's too late.

So why do attorneys—perhaps more than many other professionals—need a dedicated financial literacy guide? Let's break it down.

1. Law School Delays Financial Growth

The average attorney enters the workforce several years behind their peers in other industries. While friends in finance or tech may have started saving and investing in their early twenties, you were still in school, taking on six figures of debt, preparing for the bar, or clerking for a modest salary.

Many attorneys don't start earning real money until their late 20s or early 30s. By that time, they may already be dealing with student loans, credit card debt, or pressure to match a lifestyle that reflects their "attorney status."

This delay means that every financial decision made in the early years of practice—how you repay loans, whether you start investing, how you manage cash flow—has long-term ripple effects. Without a clear strategy, it's easy to fall behind without realizing it.

2. The Income Spectrum Is Wildly Uneven

One of the biggest misconceptions about lawyers is that they all earn six figures. While some do—and some earn multiple six figures—many attorneys earn modest salaries, especially in public interest, family law, criminal defense, or early-stage private practice.

Others might have feast-or-famine income based on contingency fees, solo practice, or business cycles.

This variability makes budgeting, planning, and investing more difficult. If you're used to large swings in income, you may delay planning altogether, waiting for that "big year" that will fix everything. But time, not timing, is what builds wealth. Financial literacy gives you the tools to operate within uncertainty and still build a stable financial future.

3. You're Paid to Solve Other People's Problems, Not Yours

You advocate for others with passion and precision. You help people protect their businesses, their reputations, their families, and their freedom. But in doing so, it's easy to neglect your own financial well-being.

The reality is that many attorneys operate under chronic stress, long hours, and high demands. Between client work, court appearances, continuing education, and managing a caseload, there's little time left to track your expenses, compare investment strategies, or plan for retirement.

That's why attorneys need a system—a financial framework that doesn't require daily attention but still delivers long-term results. Without it, burnout becomes more than emotional—it becomes financial.

4. The Lifestyle Creep Is Real

There's immense pressure in the legal profession to present success. The tailored suits. The luxury car. The downtown office. The vacations that show up in firm newsletters and social feeds.

Whether you're in BigLaw or running your own boutique firm, lifestyle creep is a constant temptation. And because income can be high, the warning signs of overspending may not show up until it's too late—when taxes are due, savings are insufficient, or a major life change hits.

Financial literacy helps you live within your values, not just your salary. It helps you differentiate between real wealth (freedom, flexibility, security) and surface-level wealth (stuff, status, stress).

5. Most Financial Mistakes Are Avoidable—But Only If You Know What to Watch For

Here are just a few common mistakes I've seen attorneys make, often because no one taught them differently:

- Carrying high-interest debt while underfunding retirement
- Paying unnecessary taxes due to poor entity or investment choices
- Buying expensive whole-life insurance policies they don't need
- Signing unfavorable partnership agreements without understanding the long-term consequences
- Waiting too long to establish estate plans, trusts, or buy-sell agreements
- Lacking disability insurance or liability protection despite being a high-risk target

These mistakes aren't about intelligence—they're about awareness. A financial literacy guide gives you the knowledge to make informed decisions, ask better questions, and avoid costly errors.

6. Your Profession Comes With Unique Risks and Opportunities

Attorneys are held to high ethical standards and face professional liability exposure. You may deal with clients who challenge invoices, judges who delay cases (and therefore payments), and partners who interpret agreements differently when money's on the line.

On the flip side, you also have access to opportunities for business ownership, consulting, teaching, firm equity, and strategic tax planning—if you know how to leverage them.

Your financial plan needs to account for these realities. It should be customized to your practice type, income structure, family goals, and risk tolerance. And it should evolve as your career does.

7. The Sooner You Start, the Easier It Gets

Like compound interest, financial knowledge builds on itself. The sooner you understand how money works—how it's earned, taxed, protected, and invested—the less reactive and more confident you become.

You don't need to know everything today. But you do need to start.

That's why this book exists—not to overwhelm you with jargon, but to walk you through the steps that matter. We'll break down:

- Budgeting and cash flow planning
- Debt management and student loan strategy
- Investing and retirement planning
- Insurance and risk protection
- Tax strategies specific to attorneys
- Business structure and law firm finances
- Estate planning and wealth transfer
- Real-life case studies and decision checklists

Final Thoughts

There's no shame in not having learned this earlier. The problem isn't you—it's that the system never taught you. But now you have the opportunity to change that.

Think of this book like legal research for your financial life. You're not expected to know every answer off the top of your head—but with the right tools, questions, and frameworks, you can navigate the landscape with clarity and confidence.

Financial literacy won't just make you a better investor—it'll make you a better professional, partner, parent, and planner. It creates space for peace of mind and long-term success—on your terms.

Because you've spent your career protecting others. Now it's time to protect yourself, too.

How to Use This Book: Financial Literacy for Attorneys

This book was written to meet you where you are—whether you're a law student with debt, an associate trying to save on a starter salary, a partner managing complex taxes, or an attorney planning for retirement and legacy.

Unlike traditional finance books, this one was created with your unique career path in mind. It recognizes the long hours, the late start to earning, the unpredictable income spikes, and the pressure of keeping up appearances. It speaks your language and respects your time.

Here's how to get the most out of this book:

1. You Don't Have to Read It Cover to Cover

Each chapter is designed to stand alone. If you're dealing with student loans, jump to that chapter. If you're focused on legacy planning, skip ahead. Think of this as your personal reference guide—read what's relevant now, and come back to the rest when you're ready.

2. Use the Book as a Roadmap, Not a Rulebook

Everyone's legal career is different. Solo practitioners, in-house counsel, BigLaw associates, government attorneys, and law professors each face distinct challenges and opportunities. Use the strategies here as a guide, but always adapt them to your own values, goals, and risk tolerance.

3. Start Small, But Start Now

Many attorneys delay financial planning, waiting until they "make partner," get that big bonus, or "have time." Don't. One of the core messages in this book is that starting early—even with small amounts—can dramatically change your long-term outcome. Pick one small step after each chapter and act on it.

4. Revisit the Book as Your Career Evolves

What matters to you now will shift as your life changes. Come back to the budgeting chapter when your income increases. Reread the estate planning section when you start a family. Revisit retirement topics as you approach your 50s. This book is meant to grow with you.

5. Talk About It With Your Spouse, Colleagues, and Clients

Financial literacy isn't just a solo mission. The more attorneys normalize financial conversations, the more we all win. Share insights from this book with your spouse or partner. Use it to shape conversations with clients who ask about wealth, asset protection, or retirement. Recommend it to younger attorneys who could use guidance.

6. Take Notes, Highlight, and Personalize It

This book is a tool, not a trophy. Mark it up. Jot questions in the margins. Highlight the tips that matter. Use it as a living part of your financial planning process.

Final Thought

You earned your JD through discipline, intellect, and grit. You already have what it takes to become financially confident and independent. *Financial Literacy for Attorneys* gives you the playbook. Now it's time to put it into practice.

Let this be your guide—not just to a stronger financial portfolio, but to a more empowered, purposeful life.

Shared Struggles: What Attorneys Have in Common with Doctors, Coaches, and Athletes

High-Income Earners, Low Financial Training, and the Cost of Success Without Strategy

When we talk about attorneys, we often talk about prestige, education, specialization, and high earning potential. But these same qualities are also found in other elite professions—doctors, college coaches, and professional athletes. Each of these careers requires deep commitment, years of preparation, high levels of discipline, and often, significant sacrifice.

Yet despite all that training and performance, there's a surprising blind spot that unites them: **financial literacy**.

Doctors. Coaches. Athletes. Attorneys. All may earn top-tier incomes at various stages of their careers. Yet most of them never received even the basics of personal finance during their education or training. And that gap—between income potential and financial awareness—can lead to costly mistakes, unnecessary stress, and lost opportunities.

Let's explore the shared challenges across these professions, and why attorneys should take this comparison seriously.

1. Education Doesn't Include Financial Preparation

Doctors spend a decade learning how to diagnose and treat illness. Athletes are trained from childhood to compete at the highest levels. Coaches master leadership, scouting, and game planning. Attorneys are drilled in critical thinking, analysis, and legal precedent. Yet almost none of these career paths include even a single course on budgeting, investing, taxes, or retirement.

Financial decisions don't get easier just because you're smart. In fact, the more complex your income, contracts, or benefits become, the more dangerous it is to rely on "figuring it out as you go."

Like doctors, attorneys often delay earnings while accumulating debt. Like coaches, many lawyers operate with performance-based compensation or incentive structures. Like athletes, you may enjoy high peak earnings followed by sudden shifts, career pivots, or burnout. The complexity is real. So is the need for structure.

2. High Income Doesn't Equal Financial Security

One of the biggest misconceptions in any high-earning profession is that income equals wealth. It doesn't.

Athletes can earn millions and go broke in five years. Doctors can earn $400,000 and still live paycheck to paycheck. College coaches can receive large bonuses while carrying zero savings. And attorneys—despite six-figure salaries—often face heavy student loans, high taxes, inconsistent cash flow, and lifestyle pressures that eat into every dollar.

Why? Because without a system, money disappears. The "more money = less worry" mindset only works when that money is managed with intention.

High earners face a unique financial challenge: **the consequences of small mistakes are amplified**. A few missed tax strategies, an overextended mortgage, or a poor insurance decision can add up to tens or even hundreds of thousands of dollars over time.

That's why financial literacy isn't just helpful—it's necessary. Especially for people like you who are operating in complex, high-responsibility environments.

3. Pressure to Present "Success" Can Lead to Lifestyle Inflation

Ask any young doctor why they bought a new luxury car six months after finishing residency. Ask a college coach why they felt pressure to live in a certain neighborhood. Ask an athlete why they gave money to everyone from their old neighborhood.

The answers vary—but the root is the same: **status, identity, and perception**.

Attorneys are no different. There's often an unspoken expectation to "look the part." The suits, the watches, the travel, the house, the private school. And when income rises, spending tends to rise with it. This is called lifestyle creep—and it's especially common among high-achieving professionals who finally feel like they've "made it."

But here's the danger: lifestyle decisions made early in your career can create fixed expenses that limit your flexibility, slow your savings, and prevent you from saying yes to better opportunities later.

Financial literacy helps you live on your own terms, not according to someone else's idea of success.

4. Complex Contracts, Compensation Structures, and Legal Terms

One of the reasons many professionals feel unprepared financially is because their compensation isn't straightforward.

- Athletes deal with endorsements, incentives, and guarantees.
- Coaches navigate base pay, performance bonuses, buyouts, and deferred compensation.
- Doctors often juggle base salary, RVUs, profit sharing, and equity in private practices.
- Attorneys may earn a base, draw, contingency fees, hourly rates, profit distributions, or firm equity—sometimes all in the same year.

These structures make financial planning harder. Without clear understanding, it's difficult to project cash flow, calculate tax liabilities, or decide how much to invest.

And ironically, even though attorneys may understand legal documents better than most, **reading your own compensation agreement or insurance policy doesn't guarantee understanding your financial exposure.**

Having financial literacy means knowing not just what you're getting paid—but how to leverage, protect, and grow that income efficiently.

5. Unpredictable Career Paths and Job Volatility

While law may feel like a "safe" profession compared to sports or coaching, it still carries volatility—especially in today's economy.

- Associates may burn out before making partner.
- Solo practitioners face the ups and downs of client flow.
- Partners may experience firm buyouts, splits, or leadership disputes.
- Government attorneys may deal with budget cuts or elections.
- Legal tech and AI are already reshaping traditional career paths.

Much like coaches who can be fired after one bad season, or athletes whose careers are ended by a single injury, attorneys are not immune to sudden changes.

A good financial plan cushions you from the instability. It gives you breathing room when you need to pivot. It allows you to choose what's next, rather than reacting to what happens.

6. Spouse and Family Dynamics Add Another Layer

High-performance careers often come with irregular hours, geographic mobility, and intense emotional demands—all of which affect personal relationships.

Attorneys, like doctors and coaches, often have spouses who are not involved in the financial decision-making or who are left in the dark. If something happens to you—an illness, a death, a disability—does your family know how to access accounts, pay bills, file claims, or continue your business?

Financial literacy is not just about protecting you—it's about protecting your family. That's something every professional should take seriously, regardless of income.

7. The Opportunity to Build Generational Wealth Is Real

Here's the good news: attorneys, like athletes, doctors, and coaches, have the capacity to build **not just income—but wealth**.

With the right systems in place, you can:

- Pay off student loans without sacrificing retirement
- Build a real estate or investment portfolio
- Protect your family with smart insurance
- Reduce taxes through better business structures
- Establish trusts, donor funds, or generational plans

You don't need to be perfect. You just need to be informed.

Final Thoughts: You Deserve the Same Strategy You Give to Others

Every day, you help clients avoid risk, protect assets, and solve high-stakes problems. You apply your expertise so they can make better decisions. But what about you?

The truth is: attorneys face the same financial gaps that plague other professionals. And in many ways, your success makes those gaps harder to see—until it's too late.

This book exists to close that gap. It's not just about information—it's about empowerment. It's your roadmap to clarity, confidence, and long-term control of your money and your future.

Because financial freedom isn't just for your clients. It's for you, too.

Let me know when you're ready for the next chapter: **"The Financial Lifecycle of an Attorney: From Law School to Legacy"** or if you'd like to include case studies of attorneys vs. other professionals who handled their finances well—or poorly.

My Background in Financial Education Across High-Income Professions

From the Field to the Boardroom—Why I Care About Teaching Smart People About Money

Before I became a financial educator and advocate, I was a college athlete chasing a dream. I played Division I football at the University of Kansas and briefly competed in the Canadian Football League. I came from a blue-collar background—hardworking parents, tight budgets, and very little financial talk at the dinner table. I knew how to work. I knew how to lead. But I didn't know how money worked.

That lack of knowledge caught up to me early. Like many student-athletes, I transitioned into adulthood with limited understanding of credit, budgeting, investing, or taxes. I took a financial literacy course in college that opened my eyes—not because it was so advanced, but because it revealed how little I truly knew. That realization changed everything.

When my football career ended, I shifted gears and became a financial advisor. I earned my MBA and dedicated myself to helping others avoid the confusion and mistakes I had faced. What started as a way to help everyday families turned into a calling to serve **high-performance professionals**—people who earn impressive incomes but often receive little to no formal education about managing it.

Over time, I built platforms and authored books specifically designed for those in complex, high-pressure careers:

- *Financial Literacy For NIL* (Name, Image, and Likeness deals for student-athletes)

- *Financial Literacy For Student-Athletes*
- *Financial Literacy For College Coaches*
- *Financial Literacy For Doctors*
- *Parents of Athletes Of Student Athletes*
- And now, *Financial Literacy For Attorneys*

Each book was born from real conversations with professionals who had *discipline, drive, and intelligence—but still felt behind financially.*

What I've learned is this: **being high-performing doesn't automatically mean being financially secure.**

Why Financial Literacy Must Be Tailored by Profession

Too often, financial advice is one-size-fits-all. You hear things like "save 10%," "don't carry credit card debt," "invest in index funds." While those rules have value, they're not designed for people with *variable income, delayed earnings, professional liability, or specialized contract structures.*

Each of the professions I serve comes with its own financial blind spots:

- **Student-athletes** suddenly making five or six figures from NIL deals without understanding taxes or budgeting.
- **Doctors** earning six figures but carrying enormous student loan burdens while receiving zero financial education during medical school.
- **College coaches** with volatile job security, performance bonuses, and incentive-based contracts—but no long-term financial game plan.
- **Attorneys,** like you, facing high earning potential, but also late financial starts, overwhelming student loans, complex income arrangements, and immense pressure to "live the part."

These challenges aren't about intelligence—they're about exposure. **No one ever taught you how to be wealthy—they just told you to work hard.** But wealth isn't the result of work alone—it's the result of what you do *with* what you earn.

That's where I come in.

What I Bring to the Table

I've spent the last two decades helping high-income professionals like you clarify their goals, protect their families, grow their wealth, and build plans that work even in the face of job changes, lawsuits, market downturns, and burnout.

I'm not just an author. I'm an advocate. I've sat down with athletes right after signing their first deal, physicians right after residency, and attorneys at every level—from first-year associates to managing partners—who looked at me and said:

> *"I make good money. But I don't feel in control of it."*

That sentence hits differently when you've heard it dozens—hundreds—of times from some of the most successful people in their fields.

The truth is: **the system isn't set up to teach you.** Your law school didn't offer personal finance electives. Your firm never explained the tax consequences of your bonus structure. No one taught you about disability insurance, estate planning, or how to read an investment statement.

That's why I've built a niche helping professionals like you learn money *the same way you learned your career*: with discipline, structure, and support.

What Financial Literacy Actually Means

To me, financial literacy isn't about memorizing definitions. It's about being able to:

- Understand where your money is going
- Make smart decisions without feeling anxious or unprepared
- Protect yourself against the downsides of success
- Set up systems that make wealth-building automatic

- Ask better questions to your CPA, advisor, and legal team
- Feel peace of mind—not just a big paycheck

It's about building a financial strategy that **reflects your values**, supports your lifestyle, and prepares you for the inevitable ups and downs of life and career.

My Work With Attorneys Specifically

While I've worked with professionals across industries, attorneys hold a unique place in my heart. Why? Because I've seen how much pressure you're under—and how much is at stake.

I've helped:

- A newly minted partner structure his compensation plan to maximize tax efficiency and avoid AMT issues
- A criminal defense attorney transition to private practice while navigating retirement account rollovers and estimated taxes
- A family law attorney buy out her previous partner while protecting her business and building a college fund for her daughter
- A solo practitioner purchase life and disability insurance to ensure her family's security if anything ever happened to her
- A litigation attorney finally tackle student loans and begin investing in a way that matched her aggressive career growth

Time after time, I see the same pattern: highly capable people simply lacking a clear, customized plan. That's why this book exists.

Why This Book Matters Now

The legal profession is evolving. Remote work, burnout, AI disruption, and generational wealth planning are all changing what it means to be a successful attorney. The old formula—billable hours + promotions =

security—just doesn't hold up anymore.

You need financial clarity. You need systems. You need advisors you can trust. And most of all, you need to believe that **financial peace is possible—even in the midst of a demanding career.**

That's what I'm here to help you build.

Final Thoughts

I didn't write this book to impress you. I wrote it to support you.

Because when your finances are under control, you can practice law with less stress, sleep better, show up more fully for your family, and make better long-term decisions.

Financial freedom isn't just about retirement. It's about **options**. It's about **clarity**. It's about never being stuck—because your money is working just as hard as you are.

You've already proven that you can handle pressure, lead others, and deliver results.

Now, let's make sure your money can say the same.

From Paycheck to Legacy: A Financial Playbook for Every Stage of Your Legal Career

Moving Beyond Survival Mode to Build Something That Lasts

Many attorneys enter the profession with one main financial goal: make enough money to pay the bills, pay off student loans, and maybe enjoy a vacation or two. And with good reason—law school debt, delayed earning years, and high-pressure jobs often make just *keeping up* feel like a win.

But at some point, the question shifts from "Am I making enough?" to "Am I building anything that will last?"

This book is here to help you make that shift—from paycheck-focused to **legacy-focused**. Because as an attorney, you have the power not only to earn a strong income—but to turn that income into impact, security, freedom, and generational wealth.

Let's talk about how.

The Problem with a Paycheck Mentality

There's nothing wrong with earning a great living. But if your financial mindset stops at the paycheck, you stay stuck in a reactive cycle: make money, spend money, repeat. That's how even six-figure earners end up with no savings, high stress, and no plan for the future.

Paycheck thinking looks like this:

- Measuring success only by monthly income

- Using bonuses or raises to justify lifestyle upgrades
- Avoiding long-term planning because "I'm doing fine for now"
- Being surprised by taxes, emergencies, or income dips
- Confusing cash flow with financial health

Eventually, this way of operating catches up with you—especially in a profession where job security can be tied to politics, performance, or firm dynamics. That's why we're going to build you a playbook that works **through every stage of your legal career**.

Stage 1: Law School and Early Career (Debt, Discipline, Foundation)

Your legal career starts in the red. Most attorneys graduate with six figures of student debt, little savings, and minimal exposure to personal finance. This stage is about building habits, not wealth. Your goal here is to:

- Understand your loan repayment options (IBR, PAYE, refinancing)
- Create your first real budget (even if it's tight)
- Start tracking your credit and building a score
- Open a Roth IRA or workplace retirement plan—even with small contributions
- Avoid lifestyle inflation when that first real paycheck hits

It's tempting to act like the money will always be there. But the real power at this stage isn't how much you earn—it's how you handle what you have.

Stage 2: The Climb (Growth, Complexity, Pressure)

This is the phase where income rises and so do the stakes. You may make partner, take on leadership roles, or open your own practice. You're earning more than ever, but now you're managing:

- Higher taxes
- Business or practice expenses
- Insurance needs
- Aging parents or growing children
- The desire for a higher lifestyle

This is where many attorneys plateau—comfortable income, but no plan beyond that. The key here is shifting from **working for your money to making your money work for you**.

At this stage, your financial playbook should include:

- A structured investing strategy (not just saving—investing)
- Tax planning to reduce your annual liability
- Term and disability insurance to protect your income
- Estate documents (will, power of attorney, health care directive)
- A relationship with a fiduciary financial advisor and CPA
- Automated savings and a cash reserve for volatility

Stage 3: Mid-Career Reevaluation (Burnout, Pivots, Priorities)

For many attorneys, there comes a moment—after 15 or 20 years of practicing—where they begin to ask deeper questions.

- Do I want to keep working like this forever?
- What's the point of all this money if I have no time?
- What happens if I get sick, burned out, or simply want to do something else?

This stage is about *reclaiming agency* over your career and finances. You start designing your financial life around your values, not just your job title.

The financial playbook here includes:

- Assessing your FIRE number (financial independence/retire early)

- Exploring income from consulting, writing, teaching, or non-legal work
- Scaling back work without scaling back lifestyle
- Investing in real estate or passive income vehicles
- Planning your ideal retirement date (and reverse-engineering the math)
- Revisiting insurance and estate plans as assets grow

Legacy-focused attorneys use this phase to shift from "making it" to "maximizing it."

Stage 4: Late Career and Exit Planning (Preservation, Impact, Legacy)

Eventually, every attorney faces an exit—voluntary or not. Whether you sell your practice, retire from the firm, or pivot to another field, you need a plan.

This stage is about protecting what you've built and transferring it with intention.

Key pieces of the playbook include:

- Creating a retirement income plan (401(k), IRA, annuities, rental income)
- Selling or transitioning your law firm/business
- Updating trusts, beneficiary designations, and charitable giving vehicles
- Gifting strategies for children or grandchildren
- Creating a family financial playbook so your spouse or heirs aren't left in the dark
- Considering long-term care, insurance needs, and healthcare planning

Legacy isn't just about leaving money—it's about leaving clarity, stability, and structure.

The Psychological Shift: Identity Beyond Your Career

One of the hardest parts of transitioning from paycheck to legacy is letting go of identity that's tied to your profession. For many attorneys, work *is* who they are.

But true financial freedom gives you the option to step away, slow down, or shift focus—without fear. That freedom is only possible when your financial life is strong, structured, and aligned with your deeper values.

You are more than your billable hours. And your legacy is bigger than your paycheck.

Putting It All Together: Your Legal Career as a Wealth Journey

Let's reframe your legal career not just as a job—but as a **financial journey**. Each phase brings different opportunities, risks, and responsibilities. But no matter where you are today, it's never too late to build a plan.

This book will walk you through:

- How to manage money smarter at every career stage
- How to reduce tax drag and protect what you earn
- How to build wealth strategically—not randomly
- How to prepare for the unexpected (divorce, disability, downturns)
- How to create an estate plan that reflects your values
- How to communicate with your family so they're prepared
- And how to build a life that's not just rich—but truly wealthy

Final Thoughts

This isn't about being perfect. It's about being prepared. Attorneys who thrive financially don't do so because they make fewer mistakes—they do so because they follow a system.

You already know how to build arguments, advocate for others, and think critically.

Now it's time to do that for yourself.

Let's build a legacy that's bigger than the work. Let's turn your income into independence—and your experience into a story that lasts far beyond your time in the courtroom.

It starts with awareness. It grows with strategy. And it ends with freedom.

Let's get to work.

Part 1: The Foundation – Law School & Early Career

Laying the Groundwork for Financial Success Before the Big Paychecks Roll In

Your financial future doesn't start when you make partner—it starts right now. Whether you're a 3L preparing for the bar exam or a newly minted associate in your first year at a firm, the financial decisions you make in these early years will shape the next 30.

The truth is, most attorneys begin their careers financially behind. Law school delays income, accelerates debt, and teaches almost nothing about personal finance. That combination makes the early career stage one of the most important—and most overlooked—parts of the financial lifecycle.

But this is also the stage where the right habits, systems, and awareness can set you up for long-term freedom, not just short-term survival.

Let's walk through the foundational elements you need to build a strong, sustainable financial life—starting now.

1. Understand Your Student Loan Landscape

Most law school grads carry significant debt—often over $100,000. And yet, many graduates don't fully understand their repayment options, interest rates, or long-term strategies.

This is the time to do a full review:

- **Know what type of loans you have** (federal vs. private).
- **Understand repayment options**: Standard, Graduated, Income-Based Repayment (IBR), PAYE, REPAYE, and PSLF.
- **Track interest rates and how much interest is accruing daily.**
- **Know when your grace period ends** and when your payments start.

If you're working for a nonprofit or government agency, **Public Service Loan Forgiveness (PSLF)** could be an option—assuming you stay in the qualifying sector for 10 years. If you're in private practice, refinancing at a lower rate could make sense once you have stable income.

Bottom line: don't ignore your loans. You don't need to eliminate them right away—but you do need a plan.

2. Build a Budget That Reflects Real Life

Law school teaches you how to analyze, write, and research—but not how to budget. And early-career lawyers are especially prone to lifestyle inflation. You've worked hard, sacrificed, and now you're finally getting paid. It's tempting to upgrade everything—apartment, car, wardrobe, dinners out.

But this is the most critical time to establish spending discipline.

A good starting budget allocates:

- **50% to needs** (housing, utilities, groceries, transportation, minimum debt payments)
- **30% to wants** (restaurants, shopping, subscriptions, travel)
- **20% to financial goals** (savings, investments, extra loan payments)

This is also the time to:

- Track your expenses for 60–90 days
- Build a basic emergency fund ($1,000 to start, with a goal of 3–6 months of expenses)
- Use tools like Mint, YNAB, or a spreadsheet to stay organized

Remember: You're not budgeting to restrict your life. You're budgeting to *build* your life.

3. Start Investing Early—Even If It's Just a Little

The earlier you start investing, the more time compound interest has to work for you.

Let's say you invest just $200/month starting at age 27. If you earn an average 7% return, you'll have over $500,000 by the time you're 60.

Start with your workplace 401(k), 403(b), or Solo 401(k) if you're a solo practitioner. Contribute enough to get any employer match—**it's free money**. Then explore Roth IRAs or taxable brokerage accounts.

At this stage, keep it simple:

- Invest in low-cost index funds or target-date retirement funds.
- Don't try to "beat the market" or time your entries.
- Stay consistent. Don't stop investing when the market dips.

The goal isn't to get rich quick. It's to get rich slowly and predictably.

4. Protect Your Income with the Right Insurance

Early-career attorneys often overlook insurance—until they need it.

- **Disability Insurance**: Your ability to earn is your most valuable asset. If an accident or illness prevents you from working, you'll still need to pay loans, rent, and bills. Get **own-occupation** coverage that applies specifically to your legal specialty.
- **Term Life Insurance**: If you have a spouse, partner, or dependents who rely on your income, get term life insurance—10 to 30 years of coverage. Avoid expensive whole-life policies unless you understand their structure and fees.
- **Renter's or Homeowner's Insurance**: Protect your belongings,

especially in a high-theft or disaster-prone area.

- **Health Insurance**: Whether through your employer or the marketplace, make sure you have adequate health coverage with an out-of-pocket maximum you can manage.

These protections are about one thing: **keeping your financial plan alive, even if life throws a curveball.**

5. Open the Right Financial Accounts and Start Organizing

Set up your financial infrastructure now, before things get more complicated:

- **Checking account** for everyday spending
- **High-yield savings account** for your emergency fund
- **Retirement account** (401(k), IRA)
- **Credit card** with no annual fee, paid in full monthly to build credit
- **Student loan portal login** with automatic payments

Consider setting up:

- A **password manager** to store login info securely
- A **shared file or document** with your partner or spouse with key financial information
- A folder or cloud storage for pay stubs, tax returns, insurance policies, and legal docs

These habits make future planning much easier and reduce the risk of missing important details.

6. Establish a Relationship with a CPA or Financial Advisor (If Needed)

You may not need a full-time financial advisor right away—but getting a CPA to help you with your taxes (especially if you're self-employed or have side income) can help you avoid early mistakes.

If you do hire a financial advisor, make sure they are:

- A **fiduciary** (legally required to act in your best interest)
- **Transparent about their fees** (flat fee or fee-only is usually best)
- **Experienced with professionals** or attorneys specifically
- **Not just selling insurance or annuities**—you want guidance, not a pitch

7. Think Ahead, Even If It Feels Premature

Even in your first year, start thinking about your future:

- Where do you want to live long-term?
- Do you want to buy a home or rent for flexibility?
- What kind of lifestyle are you building toward?
- Do you want to start a firm, go in-house, or reach partner?

You don't need all the answers. But having a vision—even a rough one—makes financial planning more intentional.

Final Thoughts: Start Where You Are, Use What You Have

The early stages of your career can feel like a whirlwind—long hours, steep learning curves, and enormous pressure to perform. But amid all that, you can still take control of your finances.

Don't wait until you "have more money" or "have it all figured out." Start with what you have now.

Because what you build in these early years—habits, systems, clarity—will either support or sabotage everything that comes next.

Let this be the season where you lay a foundation not just for a successful legal career, but for a financially secure, purpose-driven life.

Chapter 1: The Cost of Becoming a Lawyer

Understanding Debt, Planning Ahead, and Reclaiming Your Financial Power

Becoming an attorney comes with prestige, professional influence, and the promise of a strong income. But for many, it also comes with one of the heaviest financial burdens of any professional track: **student debt**.

The cost of a law degree—tuition, living expenses, bar exam preparation, lost income from delayed work years—adds up fast. And for most new lawyers, the numbers are sobering.

According to the American Bar Association, the average law student graduates with over **$160,000 in student loans**, and for those attending private institutions or out-of-state programs, the number can climb even higher.

But debt doesn't have to define your future. The key is understanding what you owe, how it works, and the strategies available to repay it in a way that fits your goals—not someone else's.

This chapter will walk you through how to get clarity on your loans, evaluate your repayment options, and avoid common mistakes that leave too many attorneys financially overwhelmed in their first decade of practice.

The Real Cost of Law School

Let's break it down:

- **Tuition**: Law school tuition can range from $25,000 to $70,000+ per year, depending on the institution and whether you qualify for in-state rates.
- **Living Expenses**: Rent, food, transportation, insurance, and other living costs typically add another $20,000 to $30,000 annually.
- **Bar Exam Prep**: Test prep, bar application fees, and the cost of surviving during the bar study period (often without full-time work) add $5,000–$10,000 more.
- **Opportunity Cost**: By attending law school, you delay earning income by three or more years—potentially missing out on $150,000+ in early-career earnings.

When it's all said and done, law school can cost over **$250,000**, especially when interest on your student loans begins accruing.

That number can feel overwhelming—but understanding it is the first step to building a plan.

Know Your Loans: Federal vs. Private

Before you can manage your debt, you need to understand what kind you have. Log into the **Federal Student Aid website (studentaid.gov)** and get a complete picture of your federal loans. For private loans, gather statements from your lenders.

Federal Loans

- Most common types: **Direct Unsubsidized Loans** and **Grad PLUS Loans**
- Key benefits:

- Income-driven repayment (IDR) options
- Potential for forgiveness (e.g., Public Service Loan Forgiveness or PSLF)
- Forbearance and deferment options
- Fixed interest rates

Private Loans

- Issued by banks, credit unions, or other private lenders
- Typically have **less borrower protection**
- No forgiveness options
- May offer lower interest rates *after refinancing,* but terms vary

If you don't know your loan types, interest rates, or total balances, now is the time to get organized. A spreadsheet or simple loan tracking app can help you stay on top of it all.

Interest Accrual and Capitalization

One of the most overlooked aspects of student loans is **interest accrual**—especially during school, grace periods, or deferment.

- **Accrual** means interest builds up daily on your loan balance.
- **Capitalization** means that unpaid interest is added to your loan's principal, creating a higher balance that future interest is then calculated on.

This is why many lawyers graduate with loan balances higher than the amount they originally borrowed.

Tip: If you're able, making small payments during law school or the grace period—just enough to cover interest—can prevent capitalization and keep your total debt lower in the long run.

Repayment Strategy: The Big Picture

Once repayment begins, you'll need to decide on a plan. Your best choice depends on your loan type, income level, career goals, and whether you work in the public or private sector.

1. Income-Driven Repayment (IDR) Plans

These plans cap your monthly payments based on your income and family size. They can make repayment more manageable early in your career and lead to forgiveness after 20–25 years.

Common options include:

- **PAYE (Pay As You Earn)**
- Monthly payment: 10% of discretionary income
- Forgiveness after 20 years
- Must have taken out loans after October 2007
- **REPAYE (Revised Pay As You Earn)**
- 10% of discretionary income
- Forgiveness after 25 years (for graduate school borrowers)
- Interest subsidies for lower-income borrowers
- No spousal income exclusion
- **IBR (Income-Based Repayment)**
- 10%–15% of discretionary income
- Forgiveness after 20–25 years
- Available for borrowers with older loans

These plans are **especially helpful in the early years** when your income is lower relative to your debt. However, keep in mind that unless you pursue PSLF, the forgiven balance at the end of the repayment term may be taxable as income.

2. Public Service Loan Forgiveness (PSLF)

If you work for a government agency or qualifying nonprofit, **PSLF** can offer complete forgiveness after just **10 years (120 qualifying payments)**—tax-free.

Requirements include:

- Having **federal Direct Loans**
- Being on a **qualifying income-driven repayment plan**
- Working **full-time** at an eligible employer
- Making **on-time payments for 10 years**

Important: Keep meticulous records. Submit the **Employment Certification Form** annually to track your progress and avoid errors in your PSLF eligibility.

PSLF can be an incredibly valuable tool for attorneys in public defense, legal aid, policy work, or government roles.

3. Refinancing

If you have a stable income, strong credit, and no plans to pursue forgiveness, refinancing your student loans through a private lender can lower your interest rate—saving you thousands over the life of your loans.

However, refinancing federal loans with a private lender means **you give up federal protections**—including deferment, forbearance, and IDR plans.

Best for:

- Attorneys in the private sector
- Those with predictable income and emergency savings
- Those who don't qualify for or need PSLF

Tip: Shop rates from multiple lenders, and avoid variable rates if you're risk-averse.

What Not to Do

- **Don't ignore your loans** hoping they'll go away. Interest will continue to grow.
- **Don't delay planning** until after your grace period ends. Start early.
- **Don't rely on forgiveness without confirming eligibility.**
- **Don't refinance federal loans without fully understanding the trade-offs.**

Final Thoughts: Make Your Degree Work for You

Your law degree is an investment—but it's only a good one if you manage the financing smartly.

The good news? You have options. And while the debt may feel like a weight, it doesn't have to hold you back. With the right plan, you can eliminate student loans systematically while still building wealth, protecting your income, and creating a life on your terms.

Remember: student loans are just one chapter of your financial journey. Don't let them define the story.

Chapter 2: Budgeting on a Starter Salary

Building a Smart Spending Plan Before the Big Paychecks Roll In

The moment your first post-law school paycheck hits your account, it can feel like a long-awaited reward. After three years of grinding through classes, clinics, and exams—possibly while racking up six-figure debt—finally getting paid feels like hitting the big leagues.

But here's the hard truth: for most new attorneys, that first salary is **just enough to feel comfortable**, and **not enough to live like you're already successful**.

Whether you're starting in public interest, clerking, or landing a modest BigLaw salary in a high-cost city, your early-career income must stretch to cover a lot: rent, food, transportation, student loans, bar prep debt, bar dues, and new wardrobe costs. Add to that the social pressure to "look like a lawyer," and it's no wonder many attorneys find themselves stressed or overspending early on.

This chapter will help you create a simple, intentional budget that allows for success without stress. It's not about restriction—it's about **building a sustainable financial rhythm** that protects your future and your peace of mind.

Step One: Face the Numbers

Start with your **actual take-home pay**—not your gross salary. After taxes, retirement contributions (if any), and insurance deductions, most attorneys take home significantly less than their advertised salary.

Example:

A $75,000 salary in a high-tax city may result in a take-home pay of around $4,500/month after deductions.

Now list your essentials:

- **Rent** (aim for no more than 30% of take-home pay if possible)
- **Utilities & internet**
- **Groceries**
- **Transportation (car, gas, public transit)**
- **Loan payments (or plan for them if in grace/deferment)**
- **Minimum credit card or other debt payments**
- **Bar-related expenses** (if still upcoming or on a payment plan)

Whatever's left goes toward discretionary spending, savings, and extra debt payments.

Step Two: Budget for Bar-Related Expenses

Many new attorneys underestimate the cost of bar admission. Even after passing the exam, you'll face:

- **Bar prep course payments** (often $1,500–$4,000)
- **Bar application fees** ($400–$1,000+)
- **Character and fitness documentation**
- **Bar dues and license fees** (typically annual, varies by state)
- **Continuing Legal Education (CLE)** costs (required in most jurisdictions)

Tip: Set aside **$100–$200/month** in a "bar fund" to stay ahead of these costs. Some employers reimburse bar fees, so ask about this during onboarding.

Even if you already passed and paid, don't forget: **CLEs and license renewals are recurring**. Build them into your long-term financial plan.

Step Three: Live Lean, Save Smart

You don't need to live like a broke student forever—but continuing to **live like a student for one more year** while earning a salary can dramatically change your financial future.

Here's how:

Build an Emergency Fund

Start with a goal of **$1,000**, then work toward **1–3 months of expenses**. Emergency funds are not for planned spending—they're your "life happens" safety net. Think: car repair, medical expense, or job disruption.

Put it in a **high-yield savings account**, not your checking account or a low-interest bank. Automate transfers—even $50–$100 a month adds up.

Avoid the New Job Spending Spree

You'll be tempted to upgrade your apartment, buy new suits, eat out more, or treat yourself for surviving law school. And some of that is okay—but **only after your budget and savings plan are in place**.

Reward yourself within reason—but don't finance your validation.

Step Four: Design a Starter Budget That Works

Use the 50/30/20 framework as a starting point:

- **50% Needs**: housing, food, transportation, loan minimums
- **30% Wants**: restaurants, subscriptions, travel, clothes
- **20% Financial Goals**: emergency savings, debt paydown, investing

On a $4,500 monthly take-home, this means:

- ~$2,250 to cover fixed needs

- ~$1,350 for lifestyle spending
- ~$900 for savings and debt reduction

If your needs consume more than 50%, adjust lifestyle spending—not savings.

Tools that help:

- Apps: YNAB, Monarch Money, Rocket Money
- Spreadsheets: simple Excel or Google Sheets budget tracker
- Bank alerts: Set up account balance notifications to monitor spending habits

Step Five: Avoiding "Lawyer Lifestyle Inflation"

This is the biggest threat to your financial freedom. You feel like you've "made it," so you spend like you've made it forever.

The problem? That suit, that new car, that dinner—it all adds up. And in five years, you might still have debt, no emergency fund, and no plan for retirement.

Common triggers of lifestyle inflation:

- Comparing yourself to senior associates, partners, or peers
- Wanting to match your firm's "image"
- FOMO on weekend trips, weddings, or luxury items
- Believing "I'll make more later" so it's okay to spend now

The truth? If you can't manage $75,000 well, you won't magically be better with $175,000.

Discipline with your starter salary creates freedom with your future salary.

Step Six: Set Financial Milestones in Year One

Give your budget purpose. Set simple but powerful goals for your first year:

- Build a $3,000 emergency fund
- Pay down your bar prep loan or first credit card
- Start investing 5% into a Roth IRA or workplace 401(k)
- Track spending for 3 full months
- Automate all your bills, savings, and debt payments

These small wins add up—and build confidence and clarity with your money.

Final Thoughts: It's Not About How Much You Earn—Yet

You don't need to be making $200,000 a year to start acting like someone who builds wealth. Budgeting is not about limiting your fun—it's about **prioritizing your freedom**.

The money you manage well in your first year as an attorney matters more than you think. You're setting a tone, creating habits, and laying a foundation that will carry you through the next 30 years of your career.

You've already proven that you have the discipline to become a lawyer. Now use that same focus to manage your financial life like a pro.

Budgeting on a starter salary is where true financial power begins—not when your paycheck doubles.

Chapter 3: Your First Real Paycheck

How to Understand, Maximize, and Build Wealth from Day One

That first real paycheck after law school is a rite of passage. For many new attorneys, it marks the beginning of financial adulthood. You've earned your degree, passed the bar, landed the job—and now, finally, you're being paid for your expertise.

But as exciting as that first paycheck is, it's also the moment when your financial literacy must go from "theory" to "practice." How you understand and use your income in the first 1–3 years of your legal career will influence your ability to save, invest, reduce debt, and eventually build long-term wealth.

This chapter will help you make sense of your paycheck, understand your compensation structure, take full advantage of your benefits, and start contributing toward retirement early—even on a modest salary.

How to Read and Evaluate Your Paycheck

It's tempting to look at your gross salary and assume that's what you'll take home. But by the time taxes, deductions, and contributions are removed, your actual paycheck tells a different story.

Let's break it down:

1. Gross Pay vs. Net Pay

- **Gross pay** is your full salary before taxes and deductions.
- **Net pay** is your actual take-home income, after all withholdings.

Example: A $100,000 salary might result in around $65,000–$70,000 in take-home pay after taxes, depending on your state, filing status, and benefits selections.

2. Key Line Items to Understand on Your Pay Stub

- **Federal income tax**: Based on your taxable income and IRS withholding tables.
- **State and local tax**: Depends on your location—high in some states (like CA or NY), nonexistent in others (like TX or FL).
- **Social Security and Medicare (FICA)**: Combined 7.65% of your salary.
- **Health insurance premium**: Deducted if you enroll in your employer's plan.
- **Retirement contributions**: If you're contributing to a 401(k) or similar plan, this will reduce your taxable income.
- **Other deductions**: Includes disability insurance, life insurance, legal dues, parking, transit, etc.

3. Always Ask:

- Is my withholding correct for my filing status?
- Are my deductions pre-tax or post-tax?
- Am I enrolled in benefits that I'm not using?
- Am I contributing enough to take full advantage of employer matches?

Keep digital or paper copies of your pay stubs for at least one year in case you need them for tax preparation or disputes.

Salary vs. Bonus Structures

Your compensation may include more than just a base salary. Many legal jobs—especially in private practice—include variable pay through bonuses or incentives. Understanding these structures is crucial for budgeting and long-term planning.

Types of Bonus Structures

- **Year-end bonus**: Often based on performance, billable hours, or firm profitability.
- **Signing bonus**: One-time upfront bonus, usually taxable and sometimes subject to repayment if you leave early.
- **Retention bonus**: Offered to encourage attorneys to stay for a defined period.
- **Discretionary bonus**: May be offered for above-and-beyond performance but is not guaranteed.

Plan for Irregular Bonuses

- Treat bonuses as *extra,* not guaranteed income.
- Avoid using them to fund ongoing lifestyle expenses.
- Allocate portions toward:
- Emergency fund
- Debt payoff
- Investing
- One-time lifestyle upgrades (vacation, furniture, etc.)

Pro tip: Create a "bonus game plan" before the check hits your account so you don't make impulsive choices.

Understanding Benefits Packages

Benefits are a key part of your total compensation. Many young attorneys overlook or undervalue their employer-sponsored benefits because they're focused only on salary. But benefits like health insurance, retirement plans, and disability coverage can easily add thousands to your real compensation.

1. Health Insurance

Understand:

- **Premiums** (what you pay)
- **Deductibles** (what you pay before insurance kicks in)
- **Copays and coinsurance**
- **Out-of-pocket maximums**

Tip: If you're healthy and your employer offers a **High Deductible Health Plan (HDHP)** with a **Health Savings Account (HSA)**, you may be able to lower your premiums and build tax-advantaged savings for medical expenses.

2. Retirement Plans (401(k), 403(b), or 457(b))

Many firms and government employers offer retirement plans with employer matching. This is **free money** that you should never leave on the table.

- Max employee contribution for 2024: **$23,000** (plus $7,500 if over 50)
- Employer match: Often ranges from 3%–6% of your salary
- Traditional 401(k): Contributions are pre-tax, reducing your taxable income
- Roth 401(k): Contributions are after-tax, but growth is tax-free

Always contribute enough to get the full match, then consider increasing your contribution rate annually or when you get a raise.

3. Disability and Life Insurance

These benefits often come with your employer plan and are essential for protecting your income.

- **Short-term and long-term disability**: Protect you if you're unable to work due to injury or illness.
- **Life insurance**: May offer 1–2x your salary. Consider supplementing with term life coverage if you have dependents.

The Importance of Roth IRA Contributions

Even if you're contributing to a workplace retirement plan, opening a **Roth IRA** is a powerful way to grow wealth tax-free.

Why Roth IRAs Matter Early

- Contributions are made with after-tax dollars, but **earnings grow tax-free**.
- **Withdrawals in retirement are tax-free**, including growth.
- You can withdraw contributions (not earnings) at any time without penalty.
- Income limits apply, but most new attorneys qualify early in their career.

2024 Contribution Limit: $7,000 (plus $1,000 if over 50)

Even small monthly contributions—$200 or $300—can grow into six figures over your career thanks to **compound interest**.

Putting It All Together: A Sample Strategy for Year One

Let's say you make $80,000 and take home $4,800/month after taxes and deductions.

Your paycheck strategy might look like:

- **$1,600 to rent and utilities**
- **$500 to food and transportation**
- **$300 to student loans**
- **$500 to Roth IRA and/or 401(k)**
- **$300 to emergency savings**
- **$400 to lifestyle/fun**
- **$1,200 for other fixed bills, insurance, bar dues, etc.**

This sample plan builds savings, avoids overspending, and lays a foundation for long-term growth—even before you hit a six-figure salary.

Final Thoughts: Your Paycheck Is a Tool, Not a Trophy

It's easy to view your paycheck as a symbol of your success—and it is! You've worked incredibly hard to earn it. But it's also a tool—a resource that needs to be managed with clarity, purpose, and discipline.

Understanding your compensation, using your benefits, and investing even a small amount early are the building blocks of real wealth.

Don't wait until you "make more" to get serious. Financial success isn't about income—it's about what you *do* with what you earn.

Start now, and your paycheck will serve you—not the other way around.

Chapter 4: Building Wealth with a Busy Schedule

Simple, Sustainable Strategies for Lawyers Who Don't Have Time to Micromanage Money

You're working 50, maybe 60 hours a week. Deadlines, depositions, client calls, court dates. The last thing most attorneys want to do when they get home is review mutual funds, rebalance a portfolio, or deep-dive into Roth vs. Traditional IRAs.

And that's okay.

Because the truth is, **building wealth doesn't require hours of daily attention**. In fact, the most successful attorneys I've worked with don't obsess over the stock market or check their accounts every day. Instead, they build systems—simple, automated, sustainable systems—and let those systems work while they focus on their careers and their lives.

This chapter is your step-by-step guide to building wealth *in the background,* without adding another time-consuming task to your already busy plate.

1. Automate Everything You Can

If there's one financial superpower that beats all others, it's **consistency**. And the best way to stay consistent? **Automation.**

Automate:

- **Savings** to a high-yield savings account (emergency fund, short-term goals)
- **Investing** into your 401(k), Roth IRA, or taxable brokerage account
- **Bill payments** (loans, credit cards, utilities) to avoid late fees
- **Transfers** between accounts (e.g., every payday move $500 into investments)

Why automation works:

- You never forget
- You remove emotion from investing (no market timing)
- You save and invest before spending (paying yourself first)
- You stay on track even during your busiest seasons

Pro tip: Set up automatic increases. For example, have your 401(k) contribution go up by 1% every year. You'll barely notice it—but your future self will thank you.

2. Understand Asset Allocation—Without Getting a Finance Degree

Asset allocation is just a fancy term for **how your investments are divided** across different asset types. Think of it as the game plan for your money.

Main Asset Classes:

- **Stocks (Equities)**: Ownership in companies. Higher risk, higher potential return.
- **Bonds (Fixed Income)**: Loans to companies or governments. Lower risk, lower return.
- **Cash and Cash Equivalents**: Like savings accounts or money market

funds. Lowest return, but stable.

- **Real Estate and Alternatives**: Rental properties, REITs, private equity—higher complexity.

Sample Allocations:

- **Aggressive (early career)**: 90% stocks / 10% bonds
- **Moderate (mid-career)**: 70% stocks / 30% bonds
- **Conservative (pre-retirement)**: 50% stocks / 50% bonds

If you don't want to build your own portfolio, you don't have to. Many 401(k)s and IRAs offer:

- **Target-date funds** (automatically adjust allocation as you age)
- **Robo-advisors** (automated investing platforms that manage allocation for you)

As long as you're contributing consistently, it's better to be **invested imperfectly** than to be sitting in cash waiting to learn everything.

3. Avoid the 5 Most Common Investment Mistakes Lawyers Make

Busy attorneys often fall into one of these traps—not from malice or laziness, but simply because they've never been shown another way.

Mistake #1: Not investing at all

Waiting until you "understand everything" or "make more money" means missing years of compound growth.

Mistake #2: Sitting on too much cash

Yes, you need an emergency fund. But beyond that, cash loses value to inflation over time.

Mistake #3: Chasing hot tips or trendy investments

Cryptocurrency, day trading, meme stocks—none of these should be the core of a lawyer's portfolio.

Mistake #4: Not rebalancing

Over time, your allocations drift. Rebalancing once a year keeps your risk level aligned with your goals.

Mistake #5: Letting fear (or overconfidence) dictate strategy

Smart investors stay the course during volatility—and don't try to outsmart the market every week.

The antidote to all five? **A simple, diversified, automated plan.**

4. The Power of Compound Interest and Time

Albert Einstein allegedly called compound interest the "eighth wonder of the world." Whether he said it or not, the math proves the point.

Let's say you invest **$500/month** starting at age 30:

- At 7% average return, you'll have **over $600,000 by age 60**
- Wait just 10 years to start (age 40), and you end up with **only $280,000**

Time does the heavy lifting. The earlier you start—even with small amounts—the more your money works for you.

Consistency beats intensity. A lawyer who invests $500/month for 30 years wins over a lawyer who invests $1,500/month for 10 years and then stops.

5. Keep It Simple—And Make It Automatic

Here's a simple setup for busy attorneys:

- **Emergency Fund**: 3–6 months of expenses in a high-yield savings account
- **401(k)/403(b)**: Contribute at least enough to get the full employer match (this is free money)
- **Roth IRA**: If eligible, contribute $7,000/year (2024 limit). If not eligible, consider a backdoor Roth.
- **Brokerage Account**: For additional investing once tax-advantaged accounts are maxed
- **HSA (Health Savings Account)**: If eligible, contribute and invest for healthcare costs or retirement

Use low-cost index funds or ETFs, automate your contributions, and check in once or twice a year.

You don't need to obsess. You need to be consistent.

6. When to Get Professional Help

If your financial life is starting to get more complex—or if you simply don't have the time or interest to manage it all—it's okay to hire help.

Look for a **fee-only fiduciary financial advisor** who:

- Understands high-income professionals
- Doesn't sell proprietary products
- Charges transparent fees (flat fee or AUM-based)
- Helps with tax strategies, estate planning, and career transitions

Your legal knowledge is your asset. Let someone else bring expertise to your financial plan so you can stay focused on your career and life.

Final Thoughts: Wealth Building Doesn't Require Perfection—Just a Plan

You don't need to become a full-time investor. You don't need to track every dollar or time the market perfectly. You just need to **start, automate, and adjust as you grow**.

Your job is demanding. Your time is limited. But your money doesn't care about your schedule—it will grow quietly in the background if you set it up correctly.

Let your paycheck fund your priorities. Let your systems do the work. Let your future self benefit from the discipline you put in place today.

Because in the legal profession, **time is money**—and when it comes to wealth building, that's not just a metaphor. It's your greatest advantage.

Chapter 5: Understanding Law Firm Compensation

Making Sense of How You Get Paid—So You Can Plan Smarter and Build Wealth Strategically

Compensation in the legal world isn't one-size-fits-all. In fact, it's anything but. Whether you're working in BigLaw, a regional firm, a boutique shop, or your own practice, the way attorneys are paid can vary widely depending on your role, seniority, performance, and the business model of your firm.

And understanding how you get paid—*really understanding it*—isn't just a paycheck issue. It affects your taxes, investment strategy, debt planning, risk tolerance, and long-term financial independence.

This chapter will walk you through the most common law firm compensation models, what to expect as you move through the ranks, and how to make financial decisions based on your actual income potential—not just your base salary.

1. Base Salary + Bonuses: The Starting Point

For most associate attorneys, compensation begins with a **base salary** and the possibility of **performance bonuses**.

Base Salary

- Typically guaranteed (unless the firm has financial instability)
- Paid biweekly or monthly
- Fixed and predictable—easy for budgeting and planning

Bonuses

- **Annual Bonuses**: Often tied to hitting billable hour benchmarks (e.g., 1,800–2,200 hours/year)
- **Discretionary Bonuses**: May depend on firm profitability, team performance, or individual value
- **Signing Bonuses**: Common for lateral hires, summer associates, or hard-to-fill roles
- **Retention Bonuses**: Used to keep high performers during transition periods or before partnership offers

Tip: Don't treat bonuses as guaranteed income. Use them for:

- Building your emergency fund
- Paying down student loans
- Investing in a Roth IRA or brokerage account
- Saving for future career pivots or time off

Avoid: Structuring your lifestyle around a bonus you *might not* get.

2. Profit-Sharing, Equity, and Partnership Tracks

As attorneys rise through the ranks, compensation models become more complex—and more tied to the **business performance** of the firm itself.

There are generally two types of partners:

- **Non-equity partners**: Paid a higher salary and sometimes a share of profits, but don't own part of the firm

- **Equity partners**: True owners of the firm, sharing in profits *and* liabilities

Profit-Sharing

- Usually calculated annually
- Based on firm profits, individual contributions, and seniority
- May fluctuate dramatically from year to year

Equity Compensation

- Often tied to "buying in" (more on that below)
- Includes a share of firm profits
- May also expose the partner to downside risk (e.g., covering firm losses or capital calls)

This is where the line between "employee" and "owner" begins to blur—and it's critical that attorneys **understand the difference**.

You are no longer just earning a paycheck. You're now investing in a business.

3. Buy-In and Buy-Out Structures

Becoming an equity partner usually requires a **buy-in**, where the attorney purchases ownership interest in the firm. This buy-in:

- Can range from $50,000 to $500,000+
- May be funded with savings, firm loans, or outside financing
- Often paid over a multi-year period through reductions in compensation

Buy-Outs occur when a partner retires or leaves the firm. The terms of the buy-out:

- May be based on tenure, equity percentage, or firm valuation
- Can be paid in installments
- May include restrictive covenants (e.g., non-competes)

Questions to Ask Before a Buy-In:

- How is the firm's value calculated?
- What percentage of profits will I earn?
- What are my liabilities if the firm struggles?
- What happens if I leave or retire?
- Are there exit strategies for partners?

Tip: Treat a buy-in like any major investment. Have the contract reviewed by an attorney *outside* the firm, and run the numbers with your CPA or financial advisor.

4. The Rainmaker vs. The Salaried Attorney

Not all partners are created equal. In many firms, **rainmakers**—those who bring in clients and revenue—earn significantly more than attorneys who focus strictly on casework.

Rainmakers

- May earn a percentage of revenue from the clients they originate
- Often receive larger profit shares or incentive bonuses
- Have more negotiating power within the firm
- Face more business development pressure

Salaried/Service Partners

- Focus on legal execution and managing teams
- Less emphasis on client generation
- Compensation tied to hours, internal contribution, and firm profitability

This division can create internal tension—but also opportunity.

If you're a strong relationship builder or marketer, developing rainmaker skills can *significantly* enhance your income over time. If you prefer legal craftsmanship, know that your earnings may top out lower unless you also gain equity or leadership roles.

Bottom line: Know where your strengths lie, and be intentional about where you want to go in the firm's ecosystem.

5. Understanding the Tax Implications of Your Compensation

Different types of compensation come with different tax treatments:

- **W-2 salary and bonuses**: Withholding handled by the firm, but large bonuses may push you into a higher bracket temporarily
- **K-1 income (for equity partners)**: Requires quarterly estimated tax payments; no withholding
- **Distributions or draws**: May vary month to month; require proactive cash management

If you're moving into equity, your financial life becomes more like a **business owner's** than an employee's. That means:

- Working with a CPA experienced in partnership taxation
- Tracking income and expenses more carefully
- Budgeting for irregular cash flow

6. Planning Around Irregular or Variable Income

As you ascend the ladder, your income may become:

- Less predictable
- More dependent on firm performance
- Tied to long-term incentives, such as profit-sharing or deferred compensation

To stay financially steady, you must:

- Build a larger emergency fund (6–12 months of expenses)
- Avoid committing variable income to fixed expenses (e.g., don't buy a house based on your *best* year)
- Use *conservative baselines* when budgeting
- Funnel windfalls (bonuses, profit shares) into long-term wealth-building, not lifestyle inflation

Final Thoughts: Know the Rules—So You Can Play to Win

Law firm compensation is layered, nuanced, and sometimes opaque. But the more you understand how your pay is structured—and how it changes over time—the more confident and strategic you'll be.

Whether you're an associate negotiating your first bonus, a service partner managing a team, or a rainmaker weighing a buy-in offer, every stage comes with both financial opportunities and responsibilities.

By educating yourself now, you'll avoid blind spots, maximize your earnings, and make choices that align with your personal and professional goals.

You work too hard not to fully understand how you're compensated.

Chapter 6: Solo Practice, Of Counsel, and Boutique Firms

From Counselor to CEO: Managing the Business Side of Practicing Law

There's a moment every attorney faces—sometimes early, sometimes later—when the idea of practicing independently becomes more than just a dream. Whether you're starting your own firm, joining a boutique, or serving clients in an "Of Counsel" role, you're stepping into more than just legal work. You're stepping into **business ownership.**

And while the idea of being your own boss is thrilling, the reality is this: success depends as much on your ability to manage **money, compliance, operations, and planning** as it does on your legal skill.

This chapter is your blueprint for how to handle the financial side of going solo, joining a boutique, or serving in a flexible capacity—without losing control, sleep, or your license.

1. Choosing the Right Business Structure

Before you take on your first client, you need a legal entity. Choosing the right one affects your taxes, liability, and long-term financial planning.

Common Legal Structures for Attorneys:

- **Sole Proprietorship**: Easiest to start but offers no liability protection. Generally not recommended for lawyers.
- **Limited Liability Company (LLC)**: Offers liability protection with flexible tax treatment.
- **Professional Limited Liability Company (PLLC)**: Required in some states for licensed professionals like attorneys.
- **S-Corporation**: Allows pass-through taxation and potential payroll tax savings if structured correctly.
- **C-Corporation**: Rarely used for solo firms due to double taxation.

Pro Tip: Many solo attorneys form an **LLC or PLLC** and then elect **S-Corp status** for tax purposes once revenue grows beyond $100,000/year. Talk to a CPA or business attorney familiar with law firms to determine the best fit.

2. Tracking Expenses and Claiming Tax Deductions

As a solo or small firm owner, you are now your own finance department. That means you need systems in place to:

- Track **every expense** related to your practice
- Separate personal and business finances
- Record receipts, invoices, and bank statements

Common Deductions for Law Practices:

- Office rent or home office percentage
- Legal research tools and subscriptions
- Continuing legal education (CLE)
- Bar dues and licensing fees
- Malpractice insurance
- Marketing and website costs

- Staff salaries and benefits
- Technology: software, computers, printers, phones

Avoid red flags by keeping a separate business bank account and using accounting software like QuickBooks, Xero, or a practice-specific tool like Clio or CosmoLex.

3. Retirement Accounts for Solo Practitioners

Just because you're solo doesn't mean you should neglect retirement. In fact, the flexibility of solo practice gives you **more control** over your retirement strategy than a traditional employee.

Options Include:

- **Solo 401(k)**: Allows employee and employer contributions. 2024 total limit: $69,000 if under 50.
- **SEP IRA**: Easier to set up but only allows employer contributions. Up to 25% of compensation, up to $66,000 (2024).
- **Traditional or Roth IRA**: Great for additional tax-advantaged savings.

Tip: If you're paying yourself a salary through an S-Corp, you can contribute both as employee and employer to a Solo 401(k), maximizing savings.

4. Setting Your Fees, Retainers, and Billing Model

One of the biggest mindset shifts for attorneys going solo is learning how to price their services. You're no longer billing hours for someone else—you're building a business.

Fee Structures:

- **Hourly billing**: Still standard in many practice areas. Make sure to set rates that reflect your experience and overhead.
- **Flat fees**: Useful for transactional work or defined scope services. Clients appreciate predictability.
- **Retainers**: Common in ongoing work. Clarify whether it's refundable, evergreen, or security-based.
- **Subscription models**: Emerging trend for small business counsel or fractional GC services.

Key Considerations:

- Know your "cost per hour" (what it costs you to operate each billable hour)
- Don't underprice out of fear. Price reflects value—and low rates can signal inexperience.
- Be transparent with clients, and get everything in writing.

Billing software like Clio, PracticePanther, or MyCase can help automate invoicing, time tracking, and collections.

5. Managing Client Trust Accounts and IOLTA Compliance

Handling client funds is a serious responsibility. Mismanaging trust accounts can lead to ethics violations, fines, and even disbarment.

Key Rules:

- **Never co-mingle** client funds with operating funds.
- **Use a separate IOLTA account** for client retainers and third-party funds.
- **Track every deposit and withdrawal** by client.

- **Reconcile trust accounts monthly** and keep detailed ledgers.

Even if you're solo, invest in trust-compliant accounting software. Or work with a bookkeeper trained in legal compliance.

Pro Tip: Know your state's rules cold. Each bar has specific IOLTA and recordkeeping requirements.

6. Hiring Staff and Building a Lean Team

When your practice grows, you may need help—but hiring doesn't always mean full-time.

Options:

- **Virtual assistants** for scheduling and intake
- **Contract paralegals** or freelance attorneys
- **Reception services** like Ruby or Smith.ai
- **Part-time admin help**

Before hiring full-time:

- Determine your break-even point (how many cases do you need to cover their salary?)
- Use 1099 contractors initially, but classify correctly to avoid IRS penalties
- Consider payroll software like Gusto or ADP when scaling up

Always have clear **employment agreements**, **non-disclosures**, and **conflict policies** in place.

7. Protecting Your Practice Legally and Financially

As both attorney and business owner, protection is your priority.

- **Malpractice insurance**: Non-negotiable. Tailor your policy to your practice area.
- **Business liability insurance**: Covers slips, falls, or non-legal business exposure.
- **Cyber liability insurance**: Critical if you store client data online.
- **Contracts for every vendor, contractor, and referral relationship**
- **Backup systems**: For data, communication, and disaster recovery
- **Contingency plans**: Who takes over if you're incapacitated?

Tip: Build a "practice binder" that includes:

- Business licenses
- Insurance policies
- Staff contact info
- Login credentials
- Key procedures

This allows someone to step in temporarily if needed—while keeping your clients protected and your license safe.

Final Thoughts: You're Not Just a Lawyer—You're the Business

Running a solo or boutique practice is a brave, bold step. It offers autonomy, flexibility, and the ability to build something that reflects your values.

But it also comes with responsibility. The more you treat your practice like a business—with structure, strategy, and protection—the more success (and sanity) you'll find.

Whether you're just starting out or looking to level up, remember: the legal work may be your passion—but the business side is what lets you keep doing it for years to come.

Invest in your systems. Invest in your knowledge. And never forget—you don't need to be perfect. You just need to be **proactive.**

Chapter 7: Tax Planning for Legal Professionals

Why Your Real Take-Home Pay Isn't What's on the Offer Letter

For most lawyers, the word *taxes* conjures stress. But tax planning isn't just about paperwork or scrambling in April—it's about understanding how your income is taxed *before* it arrives in your bank account, and using that knowledge to keep more of what you earn.

As a legal professional, your income may come from multiple sources: salary, bonuses, profit-sharing, consulting, rental properties, or firm distributions. You may get a W-2, a K-1, or multiple 1099s—sometimes all in the same year.

Without a solid tax strategy, it's easy to underpay, overpay, miss deductions, or get hit with penalties. In this chapter, we'll break down how attorneys are taxed, when to pay, how to plan proactively, and why a good CPA is worth every penny.

1. Understanding How Different Income Types Are Taxed

Let's start with the basics: **not all income is treated equally by the IRS.**

Common Types of Attorney Income:

- **W-2 Salary**:
- You're taxed through automatic withholdings from your paycheck. Your employer handles Social Security, Medicare, and income tax deductions. You receive a W-2 form at year-end.
- **K-1 Income (Partnership Distributions)**:
- If you're an equity partner, you receive a Schedule K-1 showing your share of firm income—even if it wasn't actually distributed in cash. You're responsible for paying taxes on that income.
- **1099 Income (Side Work or Independent Contractor)**:
- No taxes are withheld. You must calculate and pay both income tax and self-employment tax (Social Security + Medicare). This often applies to:
- Expert witness work
- CLE teaching
- Legal consulting
- Freelance writing
- **Capital Gains and Investment Income**:
- If you sell investments or earn dividends, you may owe short- or long-term capital gains taxes depending on your holding period and income bracket.
- **Rental or Real Estate Income**:
- Taxable, but offset by depreciation and expenses if managed properly.

The first step in tax planning is understanding **how each dollar is earned** and **what tax it triggers**.

2. Quarterly Estimated Payments and Business Write-Offs

If you earn **any significant non-W-2 income**, you may need to pay **quarterly estimated taxes** to avoid IRS penalties.

When It Applies:

- You're a solo or equity partner
- You receive 1099s
- You have significant investment or rental income

Due Dates:

- April 15
- June 15
- September 15
- January 15 (of the following year)

Failing to make these payments could result in an underpayment penalty—even if you eventually pay the full amount in April.

Business Write-Offs for Solos or Small Firms:

If you operate as a solo practitioner or own a firm, your tax strategy should include every legal deduction available:

- Office rent or home office expenses
- Legal research and subscriptions
- Bar dues, CLEs, and licensing
- Staff salaries and contractor payments
- Marketing and website expenses
- Professional insurance
- Travel and meals (if business-related)
- Equipment and software
- Retirement contributions (Solo 401(k), SEP IRA)

Pro tip: Use accounting software or a CPA to track deductions in real time—not just at tax time. Keep digital receipts and categorize expenses monthly.

3. Working With a CPA vs. Doing It Yourself

As your financial picture becomes more complex, working with a **Certified Public Accountant (CPA)** isn't a luxury—it's a necessity.

When DIY Might Work:

- You're a salaried W-2 attorney with no side income or investments
- You use simple tax software (TurboTax, TaxSlayer)
- You understand your deductions and standard forms

When to Hire a CPA:

- You're a partner or firm owner
- You earn K-1 or 1099 income
- You own a home, multiple accounts, or real estate
- You're planning charitable donations, stock options, or business ventures
- You want year-round planning—not just April help

Tip: Choose a CPA who works with other lawyers or high-income professionals. They'll understand:

- Deducting legal-specific expenses
- Navigating partnership tax codes
- Structuring retirement and benefits
- Handling multi-state income if you practice in multiple jurisdictions

A good CPA doesn't just fill out forms—they build a strategy that can save you thousands.

4. Tax Planning for Partnerships and Distributions

If you're an equity partner, your tax world shifts dramatically.

Key Features of Partner Taxation:

- You're taxed on **your share of the firm's profit**, whether you receive it or not.
- Income flows through to your personal return via a **Schedule K-1**.
- You must pay **self-employment tax**, unless structured otherwise through an S-Corp.
- You're likely responsible for **your own estimated tax payments**.

Things to Know:

- Distributions may be irregular. Budget accordingly.
- Retirement plan contributions are often your responsibility.
- Capital accounts and buy-ins may affect your tax exposure at exit.

If you're considering partnership or just made partner, meet with your CPA to set up a:

- Quarterly tax plan
- Payroll draw strategy (if applicable)
- Withholding adjustment (for hybrid comp)
- Retirement contribution plan
- Budget for annual tax surprises

You're now running a business. Treat it like one.

5. Planning for Side Gigs (Teaching, Consulting, Expert Witness Work)

Side income is common for attorneys—but it often brings surprises at tax time.

Common Pitfalls:

- No taxes withheld on 1099 income
- Underestimating self-employment tax
- Not tracking related expenses
- Forgetting quarterly payments

What You Can Deduct:

- Travel and lodging for speaking gigs
- Home office expenses (if used exclusively for side work)
- Supplies, marketing, or subscriptions used for your side business
- Legal or accounting fees tied to side ventures

Entity Structure:

- For modest side work, you can operate as a sole proprietor.
- For recurring or larger income, consider forming an **LLC** and electing **S-Corp** status to reduce self-employment tax.

Pro tip: Open a separate bank account for side income. This keeps things clean, clear, and IRS-ready.

Final Thoughts: The IRS Doesn't Care That You're Busy

Tax planning isn't about being perfect—it's about being proactive.

The more you earn, the more tax planning matters. But you don't have to do it all yourself. What you do need is a system: a clear understanding of how you're paid, a professional team if needed, and a strategy that keeps more money working for you—not just paying the government

Taxes aren't just an annual annoyance—they're one of the biggest costs in your financial life.

Learn to manage them well, and your wealth will thank you.

Chapter 8: How Compound Interest Builds Wealth While You Work

Compound interest is often called the eighth wonder of the world. Why? Because it can turn a little money saved consistently into a large sum over time—all while you're busy practicing law, managing clients, and living life. In this chapter, we'll break down exactly how compound interest works, why it's especially valuable for attorneys, and how to visualize its impact on your financial future.

What Is Compound Interest?

In the simplest terms, compound interest is interest that earns interest. Instead of just earning interest on the money you invest (called your "principal"), you also earn interest on the interest you've already earned. This cycle continues, creating a snowball effect that accelerates wealth over time.

Simple Interest vs. Compound Interest

Let's compare:

- **Simple Interest**: You invest $10,000 at 5% interest for 5 years. You earn $500 per year. After 5 years, you have $12,500.
- **Compound Interest**: You invest $10,000 at 5% interest, compounded

annually. After 5 years, you have **$12,763**.

The difference grows bigger the longer you stay invested.

The Math Behind Compounding (Don't Worry, It's Simple)

Here's the basic compound interest formula:

A = P(1 + r/n) ^ nt

Where:

- **A** = final amount
- **P** = principal amount (your original investment)
- **r** = annual interest rate (decimal form)
- **n** = number of times interest is compounded per year
- **t** = number of years invested

Even without crunching numbers, the key takeaway is: **the earlier and more often you invest, the more your money grows**.

Visualizing the Growth

Let's say you invest $5,000 a year starting at age 25 and stop at age 35—just 10 years. Your total contributions would be $50,000.

Now compare that to someone who starts saving $5,000 a year at age 35 and continues until age 65. They contribute $150,000.

Assuming an 8% return:

- The early saver ends up with **$602,000**
- The later saver ends up with **$540,000**

You read that right: the person who saved less money ends up with more wealth.

Why Compound Interest Matters for Attorneys

As an attorney, your schedule is demanding. You may not always have the time or mental space to actively manage your finances. That's what makes compound interest so powerful: **it works for you while you're busy working for others.**

If you consistently set aside money and invest it, compound interest becomes your financial teammate. It doesn't need a promotion, a billable hour, or a law degree. It just needs time.

The Rule of 72

Want a quick estimate of how long it will take to double your money?

Use the Rule of 72:

72 ÷ annual interest rate = years to double your investment

For example:

- 72 ÷ 6% = 12 years
- 72 ÷ 8% = 9 years
- 72 ÷ 10% = 7.2 years

If you invest at an 8% average return, your money will double roughly every 9 years. That means $25,000 becomes $50,000… then $100,000… then $200,000… all by staying invested.

Where to Use Compound Interest

1. Roth IRA

- Contributions grow tax-free
- You never pay taxes on withdrawals in retirement

2. 401(k)

- Pre-tax contributions reduce your taxable income now
- Growth is tax-deferred until you withdraw it later

3. Brokerage Account

- Fully flexible for mid-term or long-term investments
- Great for those who have maxed out their retirement accounts

Start Early. Stay In. Let It Grow.

The most important lesson with compound interest is this:

Start early. Stay invested. Don't interrupt the process.

Don't panic when the market dips. Don't pull your money out because of a bad news headline. Compound interest requires time and patience, not timing the market.

Real-Life Attorney Example

Meet Sandra, a 28-year-old associate who saves $200/month in a Roth IRA. She never increases the amount but stays consistent.

At 8% growth, by age 65, her account grows to **$589,000.** She only contributed $89,000 over the years.

Now imagine she increases that to $500/month at age 35. She contributes more—$180,000 total—but ends up with **$745,000**.

More money, yes. But had she started sooner with smaller amounts, she would have had even more.

Final Word

Compound interest is the reward for financial discipline. It's the silent engine behind your future wealth.

If you understand nothing else about investing, understand this: **compound interest is your best friend.**

Start saving. Stay invested. Let time do its thing.

Because one day, while you're arguing a case, writing a brief, or even taking a sabbatical, your money will be working quietly in the background—growing, compounding, and giving you the financial independence you deserve.

Part 2: Mid-Career Moves – Growing Income, Growing Responsibility

F*rom Stability to Strategy: Leveraging Your Earning Years for Long-Term Wealth*

Mid-career is where everything gets more real—and more complicated.

You're earning more. Your title carries weight. Your calendar is packed. And yet, despite the professional success, you might still feel like your financial life is just... okay. Not bad. But not bulletproof.

That's because mid-career is when income rises, but so do your responsibilities:

- Bigger rent or a mortgage
- Children or family planning
- Aging parents
- Taxes that eat into bonuses
- Partnership tracks, ownership stakes, or business ventures
- The looming realization that "retirement planning" isn't just for older lawyers

This stage is where many attorneys shift from *making it* to *maximizing it*. You're out of survival mode—but it's time to avoid stagnation. Mid-career is when smart decisions pay compound dividends. The habits, strategies, and structures you build now will either create long-term freedom—or lead to missed opportunities.

Let's dive into what it takes to win financially in your career's most pivotal stretch.

1. Don't Let a Bigger Paycheck Create Bigger Problems

Your income has likely grown since your early years in practice. But just because you make six figures (or more) doesn't mean you're building wealth.

In fact, many attorneys at this stage fall into what's called the **"comfort trap."**

- You're earning enough to live well…
- But not enough is going toward saving, investing, or debt reduction…
- Because your expenses have grown with your income…

This is **lifestyle inflation**, and it's a silent wealth killer.

Now is the time to ask:

- How much of your raise this year went into investments?
- Are you increasing your retirement contributions annually?
- Are you living within your means—or just at the edge of your income?

Pro move: When you get a raise, automate a percentage of it into savings and investments before you ever see it in your checking account.

2. Revisit Your Budget—Even If You Don't Think You Need To

At this stage, budgeting isn't about penny-pinching. It's about **alignment.**

You want to make sure your spending reflects your values, your goals, and your season of life.

Ask yourself:

- Am I prioritizing family, travel, real estate, giving, or early retirement?

- Am I overspending in areas that no longer bring me joy or ROI?
- Is my financial plan designed around a strategy—or just momentum?

Your cash flow has likely evolved. So should your plan. Don't let a budget written three years ago define your future priorities.

3. Get Strategic with Debt—Not Just "Aggressive"

By now, you've likely made a dent in your student loans. Maybe you've refinanced, switched repayment plans, or knocked them out altogether.

But new debt may have emerged:

- A mortgage
- Car loans
- Private school tuition
- Business or practice-related financing

The goal isn't necessarily to be 100% debt-free. It's to be **debt-smart**.

Key questions:

- Am I getting a better return on investments than I'm paying in interest?
- Is this debt helping me build assets or buy liabilities?
- Should I refinance for better terms now that my income is more stable?

Sometimes paying off low-interest debt aggressively isn't the best move. Balancing strategic investing with efficient debt management often leads to better long-term outcomes.

4. Max Out Your Tax-Advantaged Retirement Options

Mid-career is prime time to **accelerate your investing**.

You should be:

- **Maxing out your 401(k)/403(b)** ($23,000 in 2024)
- Using **Roth IRA or Backdoor Roth IRA strategies** (income limits apply)
- Exploring **Health Savings Accounts (HSAs)** if eligible
- Opening a **taxable brokerage account** for added flexibility and growth
- If self-employed or part-time, considering **SEP IRAs or Solo 401(k)s**

Bonus tip: Increase your 401(k) contributions with every raise. Even an additional 1% per year makes a difference over time.

5. Tax Planning Isn't Optional Anymore

As your income grows, so does your tax bill—and the value of **smart planning**.

Work with a **CPA who understands high-income professionals**. They can help you:

- Strategically manage bonuses and RSUs (if applicable)
- Utilize itemized deductions, including legal association dues, unreimbursed expenses, or charitable contributions
- Maximize retirement contributions and tax-loss harvesting
- Evaluate the benefits of an **S-Corp** or **LLC** structure if you have side income
- Plan for **quarterly tax payments** if your withholding isn't sufficient

Red flag: If you owe taxes every year and feel surprised each April, your plan needs work.

6. Get Serious About Insurance and Risk Management

You're in your peak income years. A serious illness, disability, or lawsuit could undo a decade of progress. It's time to review:

- **Long-term disability insurance**: Should cover 60–70% of income with "own-occupation" language.
- **Term life insurance**: Especially if you have kids, a mortgage, or dependents.
- **Umbrella liability insurance**: Covers you beyond home/auto policies if you're sued.
- **Professional liability insurance**: If you're solo or at risk for claims outside your employer's coverage.

Mid-career is when you have the most to lose—so protect it.

7. Estate Planning: No Longer Optional

You don't need to be wealthy to need a will. You need to be a responsible adult.

Now is the time to:

- Create or update your **will**
- Establish **power of attorney** (financial and medical)
- Designate **guardianship** if you have children
- Set up **beneficiary designations** and review them annually
- Explore **trusts** for privacy, control, and tax efficiency if you're building significant wealth

This is especially important for blended families, second marriages, or business owners.

8. Don't Ignore Your Career Trajectory

Mid-career is also when burnout creeps in. You might feel disillusioned, plateaued, or ready for something new.

Now is the time to:

- Reassess your 5-, 10-, and 20-year professional goals
- Explore non-billable income streams (consulting, teaching, writing)
- Consider moving toward **partnership, in-house, or self-employment**
- Protect your ability to pivot with a strong financial foundation

Your money gives you freedom—to say no to toxic environments, to take a sabbatical, to launch your own firm.

That's why financial literacy matters.

Final Thoughts: Own Your Prime Earning Years

Mid-career isn't the time to coast—it's the time to **capitalize**.

This is when your income is rising, your experience is valued, and your choices start compounding—either positively or negatively.

By mastering budgeting, investing, insurance, tax planning, and career flexibility now, you lay the foundation for long-term financial independence.

Remember: you're not working this hard just to get by. You're building something. A lifestyle. A legacy.

And this is the season to build it wisely.

Chapter 9: Automating Your Investments for Long-Term Success

Attorneys live demanding, fast-paced lives. Between billable hours, court appearances, client meetings, and ongoing professional development, managing personal finances can easily fall to the bottom of the priority list. That's why automation isn't just convenient—it's essential. In this chapter, you'll learn how to automate your investments so that you're consistently building wealth in the background, regardless of your schedule or the market's mood.

Why Automation Matters for Attorneys

Time is your most valuable asset. Automating your finances means you spend less time worrying about whether you're doing the right thing—and more time focused on your legal practice and personal life.

Automation:

- Removes emotion from investing
- Ensures consistency
- Keeps your plan on track during market ups and downs
- Helps prevent lifestyle creep

The Psychology Behind "Set and Forget"

Emotional investing is one of the biggest obstacles to wealth creation. When markets are down, fear can lead you to sell. When markets are booming, greed can cause you to over-invest. Automation helps you:

- Stay on your plan, regardless of headlines
- Avoid panic selling or irrational buying
- Benefit from dollar-cost averaging (buying more shares when prices are low, fewer when prices are high)

How to Automate Your Investments

Step 1: Set Up Direct Deposit Splits

Ask your HR department if you can split your paycheck. Send part to your checking account, and part directly to your investment or savings account.

Step 2: Automate Transfers to Investment Accounts

Use your bank or brokerage platform to automatically transfer a set amount each month into your:

- Roth IRA
- Traditional IRA
- 401(k) (via payroll)
- Brokerage account

Step 3: Automate Your Actual Investments

Many platforms let you set up automatic purchases of stocks, ETFs, or mutual funds. You can:

- Choose the fund(s) you want (e.g., S&P 500 index)
- Select the amount
- Schedule monthly or bi-weekly buys

Step 4: Reinvest Dividends Automatically

Make sure you're signed up for **Dividend Reinvestment Plans (DRIPs)** so any dividends you earn are automatically used to buy more shares. This supercharges compounding.

Best Platforms for Automation

- **Fidelity** – User-friendly, with strong automation tools
- **Vanguard** – Great for index investing and reinvestment
- **Schwab** – Offers robo-advisory options and scheduled investing
- **M1 Finance** – Known for automation and portfolio customization
- **Betterment** – Robo-advisor that handles everything automatically

How Much Should You Automate?

The rule of thumb is to invest **at least 15–20%** of your gross income for retirement. But if you're just starting:

- Begin with 5–10%
- Increase your contributions annually or with each raise
- Revisit every 6–12 months to boost your savings rate

Building Consistency Over Time

Success in investing isn't about perfect timing. It's about consistent action. Here's what you gain from automating:

- Peace of mind

- A growing portfolio without effort
- The ability to stay invested during volatility
- Protection against bad decisions

What If You Need to Pause?

Life happens—big expenses, job transitions, or emergencies. The beauty of automation is that it's easy to pause or adjust. But when you can, **restart**. The key is to avoid long gaps.

Avoiding Common Pitfalls

- Don't wait for "the right time" to start
- Don't cancel automation due to short-term fear
- Don't micromanage your accounts weekly

Remember, investing should feel **boring and consistent**. That's when it's working.

Final Thoughts

Your legal career is likely filled with high-stakes decisions. Your investing strategy doesn't have to be. Set up your accounts. Schedule your deposits. Let your investments grow quietly and consistently in the background.

Automate today, so you don't have to overthink tomorrow.

Because when you look back 10, 20, or 30 years from now, you won't remember the market dips or the media noise. You'll remember that you had a plan—and stuck to it.

Chapter 10: Saving Early – Your Most Powerful Financial Advantage

In the fast-paced world of law, where time is often quite literally money, the idea of slowing down to think about savings may seem impractical. As a young attorney, you may be laser-focused on establishing your career, paying off law school debt, and climbing the professional ladder. However, this chapter will make one thing crystal clear: **saving early is your single greatest financial advantage.**

Not your salary. Not the size of your bonus. Not even the firm you work for.

It's *time.*

When you understand how to use time to your financial advantage, you gain a superpower. One that allows you to build wealth quietly, steadily, and often effortlessly. This chapter will walk you through why early saving matters, how to start, and real-world examples showing just how powerful starting early can be — even with small amounts.

The Misconception: "I'll Start Saving When I Make More"

This is one of the most common mindsets among young professionals, especially attorneys. After years of expensive education, delayed earnings, and mounting student loans, it can feel justified to delay saving until your income increases.

But here's the truth:

If you can't save $100 out of $1,000, you probably won't save $1,000 out of $10,000.

Saving is less about how much you make and more about the habit you build.

Waiting to save until you "have more" is like waiting to get in shape until you "have more time." The longer you wait, the harder it becomes to catch up.

The Time Value of Money: How It Actually Works

The earlier you save and invest, the more time your money has to **compound.**

Compounding is what happens when the money your money earns also starts earning money. Over time, it leads to exponential growth. It doesn't just add up. It multiplies.

Simple Example:

Let's say you invest $5,000 at age 25 in a fund that earns 8% a year, and you don't touch it.

By the time you're 65, that $5,000 will grow to **$108,623**.

Now imagine you waited until age 35 to invest that same $5,000. At the same 8% return, by age 65, you'd have just **$50,313**.

By starting **10 years earlier**, you almost **double** your money, even though you didn't invest a single dollar more.

The Million-Dollar Difference: Two Attorney Scenarios

Meet Early Erin:

- Starts saving at 25
- Invests $500/month
- Stops saving at age 35 (10 years total)
- Total invested: $60,000

At age 65, Erin's account is worth **$1.04 million** (assuming 8% annual return).

Meet Late Larry:

- Starts saving at 35
- Invests $500/month until age 65 (30 years)
- Total invested: $180,000

At age 65, Larry's account is worth **$745,000**.

Erin saved for just 10 years and ends up with more money than **Larry, who saved for 30 years.** Why? Because Erin gave her money more time to grow.

The Real-World Challenge for Young Attorneys

Most new attorneys carry law school debt, face high living expenses in major cities, and work long hours that make budgeting seem impossible. But here's where perspective matters:

Even if you can only save $50, $100, or $200 a month in your early years, it *still* puts you ahead.

Starting Small Still Pays

Let's say you only manage to save $100/month starting at age 25.

- By age 65, at 8% growth, that becomes: **$349,000**

Now compare that to starting at age 35:

- Same $100/month, same return: **$157,000**

You miss out on nearly **$200,000** by delaying 10 years.

The Habits You Build Matter More Than the Amount

Early saving is about building habits:

- Automating your savings
- Learning to live on slightly less than you earn
- Prioritizing long-term goals over short-term spending

If you start saving early, you train your financial muscle. When you begin earning more later, that muscle is already strong.

Where to Save and Invest Early

Here are the best accounts for young attorneys to get started:

Roth IRA

- Funded with post-tax dollars
- Grows tax-free
- Withdrawals in retirement are tax-free
- Income limits apply (but early-career attorneys usually qualify)

Employer 401(k) or 403(b)

- Many firms offer a retirement plan with employer match
- Maximize the match — it's free money

Taxable Investment Account

- No contribution limits
- Offers flexibility for mid-term goals like buying a home or starting a firm

High-Yield Savings Account

- Great for emergency fund
- Not for long-term investing, but important to have as a safety net

Your First Steps: What You Can Do Now

1. **Start small but start now.** Even $50/month matters.
2. **Automate it.** Set up automatic transfers from checking to savings or investment accounts.
3. **Open a Roth IRA.** Consider platforms like Fidelity, Schwab, or Vanguard.
4. **Increase contributions with raises.** Every time your salary increases, raise your savings rate too.
5. **Track your net worth.** Seeing progress keeps you motivated.

Psychological Wins of Saving Early

Saving early gives you more than just financial return. It builds:

- **Confidence**: Knowing you're ahead of the curve
- **Peace of mind**: Not living paycheck to paycheck

- **Options**: Freedom to take career risks, like launching a solo firm
- **Compound wins**: Small wins now grow into huge victories later

What If You Didn't Start Early?

It's never too late to start. But if you're in your 30s or 40s reading this, you need to act with **urgency**. You may need to:

- Save more aggressively
- Cut back on expenses
- Delay big purchases
- Increase your investment contributions significantly

But don't let regret paralyze you. Let it **motivate** you.

The Bottom Line

In law, we often focus on winning the case, the client, or the argument. But when it comes to your finances, winning is about **starting early**.

You don't need a six-figure income to become a millionaire. You need a plan, consistency, and time.

Start now. Build the habit. Let time do the heavy lifting.

Because in the long game of wealth-building, the early saver almost always wins.

Action Checklist:

- Open a Roth IRA this week
- Automate a monthly transfer, even if it's just $50
- Check if your employer offers a 401(k) and match
- Download a net worth tracking app
- Set a goal: $5,000 saved by year-end

Let this be the year you stop saying "I'll save later" and start saying "I'm building wealth now."

You're not just a lawyer. You're a future millionaire in the making. Start acting like one today.

Chapter 11: Insurance Every Attorney Needs

Protecting Your Income, Practice, and Peace of Mind

Lawyers are trained to assess risk—but when it comes to their own lives and practices, many attorneys remain **underinsured** or **improperly insured**. And while insurance may not be the most exciting part of financial planning, it's one of the most important.

You've worked hard to build a career and earn a strong income. But it only takes **one unexpected event**—a malpractice suit, a car accident, an injury, or an illness—to unravel years of progress if you're not protected.

This chapter breaks down the core insurance policies every attorney should understand. Whether you're an associate at a big firm, a solo practitioner, or a partner with ownership interest, the right coverage can be the difference between **financial resilience** and **financial disaster**.

1. Malpractice Insurance: Your Professional Lifeline

If you provide legal services, you need **legal malpractice insurance**—even if you think you'll never need it.

Two Primary Types of Coverage:

- **Claims-Made Policies**
- Only cover claims **filed while the policy is active**, regardless of when the work occurred.
- Require **tail coverage** if you cancel or change providers—this extends protection for claims that arise after the policy ends.
- Most common type of coverage for lawyers.
- **Occurrence Policies**
- Cover any claim stemming from work **performed while the policy was active**, regardless of when the claim is made.
- Rare in legal malpractice insurance due to complexity and higher costs.

Key Considerations:

- **Limits of liability** (e.g., $1M per claim / $3M aggregate)
- **Deductibles** (higher deductibles can lower premiums)
- **Exclusions** (make sure your practice area is covered)
- **Consent-to-settle clauses** (you should retain control)

If you're a solo or small firm attorney, malpractice coverage is non-negotiable. Even the most careful lawyers can face a claim for missed deadlines, poor communication, or client misunderstandings.

Pro Tip: Don't just buy the cheapest policy. Buy the one that will actually protect you—and your license.

2. Disability Insurance: Protect Your Ability to Earn

Your ability to work and earn income is your most valuable asset Disability insurance protects that asset if you become too sick or injured to practice law.

Two Major Types of Coverage:

- **Own-Occupation Disability Insurance**
- Pays benefits if you can't work in **your specific profession**, even if you could work elsewhere.
- Ideal for attorneys, especially those with specialized practices.
- **Any-Occupation Disability Insurance**
- Only pays if you can't work **in any job** you're reasonably suited for.
- Often cheaper, but far less protective.

Policy Features to Consider:

- **Elimination period**: How long before benefits begin (typically 60–90 days)
- **Benefit period**: How long benefits last (e.g., 2 years, 5 years, to age 65)
- **Residual/partial coverage**: Covers partial loss of income if you return to work at reduced capacity
- **Cost-of-living adjustment (COLA)**: Increases benefits annually for inflation

Employer-provided disability insurance is a start—but it may not be enough. Coverage often ends if you leave the job, and benefits are usually taxable. Consider purchasing **a personal policy** for long-term protection.

3. Life Insurance: Providing for Others if You're Gone

Life insurance isn't for you—it's for the people you leave behind.

If you have a spouse, partner, children, or aging parents who rely on your income, life insurance is essential.

Term vs. Permanent Life Insurance:

- **Term Life**
- Covers you for a fixed period (10, 20, or 30 years)
- Simple, affordable, and ideal for most lawyers
- Provides a high death benefit at low cost
- Use it to cover specific obligations (mortgage, college, support needs)
- **Permanent Life** (Whole, Universal, Variable)
- Covers you for life
- Includes a cash value component
- Significantly more expensive
- Only makes sense for estate planning or complex financial strategies

How Much Coverage?

A general rule of thumb: **10–15x your income**
Also consider:

- Debts and mortgages
- Future education expenses
- Funeral and legal costs
- Lost income over decades

Tip: Always name primary and contingent beneficiaries and revisit them after major life changes.

4. Core Personal Insurance Policies Every Attorney Needs

Even if your professional life is covered, your personal assets also need protection.

Health Insurance

- Choose between employer-provided plans or individual coverage
- Understand premiums, deductibles, and out-of-pocket maximums
- Consider High Deductible Health Plans (HDHPs) with Health Savings Accounts (HSAs) for long-term tax benefits

Auto Insurance

- Liability coverage protects you if you're at fault
- Comprehensive/collision protects your own vehicle
- Raise liability limits if you have high income or assets

Homeowners or Renters Insurance

- Covers damage to your home and personal property
- Includes liability coverage if someone is injured on your property
- Required if you have a mortgage

Umbrella Liability Insurance

- Adds an **extra $1–5 million** of liability coverage above your auto/home policies
- Essential for high-income professionals who could be targeted in lawsuits
- Typically very affordable ($200–$400/year for $1 million in coverage)

5. Business Insurance for Solos and Small Firm Partners

If you run your own firm or share ownership in a practice, you also need to insure the **business itself**.

Must-Have Business Coverages:

- **General Liability Insurance**: Covers bodily injury or property damage at your office
- **Business Owner's Policy (BOP)**: Bundles general liability and property insurance
- **Cyber Liability Insurance**: Protects against hacking, data breaches, or lost client information
- **Employment Practices Liability Insurance (EPLI)**: Covers claims from employees regarding harassment, discrimination, or wrongful termination
- **Commercial Property Insurance**: Covers your physical office, furnishings, and equipment
- **Business Interruption Insurance**: Pays for lost income during a covered shutdown (e.g., natural disaster, fire)

If you have employees, you may also be required to carry:

- **Workers' compensation insurance**
- **State-mandated disability or paid family leave coverage**

Pro Tip: Work with an insurance broker who specializes in professional service firms to avoid gaps or duplications in coverage.

Final Thoughts: Risk Is Real—But Protection Is Power

You spent years building your career and reputation. One accident, lawsuit, or illness shouldn't be the thing that unravels it all.

Insurance doesn't eliminate risk—it transfers it. The right policies don't just protect you—they protect your family, your firm, your clients, and your future.

Make time—once a year—to review your coverage:

- Are your policies up to date?
- Do your beneficiaries need updating?
- Has your income, firm structure, or family situation changed?

Protection isn't glamorous. But in the financial game, **defense wins championships too**.

Chapter 12: Protecting Your Personal Assets

Build Wealth, But Also Build Walls Around It

You don't have to be reckless to get sued. You don't have to be wealthy to become a target. And you don't have to be guilty for a legal claim to cost you time, money, and stress.

As a legal professional, you're in a high-risk category—by profession, income level, and public exposure. Whether you're defending clients, advising high-stakes cases, or simply operating a practice, you carry an inherent amount of legal and financial liability that can follow you home.

Which is why **protecting your personal assets isn't optional—it's essential**.

You've worked hard to build wealth. In this chapter, we'll show you how to protect it through legal structures, insurance strategies, and good financial hygiene.

1. Asset Protection 101: What Are You Really Safeguarding?

Asset protection is about keeping what's yours—your home, savings, retirement accounts, investments, and business equity—from being wiped out by:

- Civil lawsuits
- Divorce settlements

- Creditor claims
- Business disputes
- Malpractice or negligence lawsuits
- Bankruptcy
- Death without a plan in place

The goal isn't to hide assets—it's to legally and ethically shield them through **proactive planning** that stands up in court and keeps your financial life intact no matter what storms come your way.

2. Trusts, Titling, and Legal Structures That Protect Wealth

Revocable Living Trusts

Used primarily for estate planning, not asset protection. They:

- Avoid probate
- Allow you to control how assets are distributed
- Do *not* protect assets from lawsuits or creditors during your lifetime

Irrevocable Trusts

- Offer strong protection—but once you put assets in, you lose control
- Often used for gifting, estate tax planning, or high-net-worth protection
- May protect assets from future lawsuits *if created in advance*

Pro Tip: Asset protection trusts should always be created by a lawyer who understands the nuances of your state's laws.

Titling Assets Strategically

- **Tenancy by the Entirety** (available in some states): Protects jointly owned property between spouses from individual creditors
- **Joint Tenancy with Right of Survivorship (JTWROS)**: Avoids probate but doesn't offer creditor protection
- **Individual vs. Joint Accounts**: Know what's exposed and to whom

LLCs and Corporations

- Use for rental properties, side businesses, or personal ventures
- Separate liability between your business and personal assets
- Keep clean books: intermingling personal and business funds can pierce the "corporate veil"

If you're earning side income, renting property, or advising clients outside of your main firm, consider forming a **single-member LLC** to compartmentalize risk.

3. Why Umbrella Insurance Is the Most Underrated Asset Protection Tool

Attorneys are often high earners *and* high visibility—which means lawsuits can get personal, even if they start with a fender bender or a guest injury at your home.

What Is Umbrella Insurance?

It's a personal liability policy that kicks in **after** your auto or home insurance limits are exhausted. It protects you from:

- Bodily injury lawsuits
- Property damage claims

- Defamation, libel, or slander suits
- Legal fees related to these issues
- Liability related to rental property or personal activities

Example:

- You're in a car accident and found liable for $1.2 million
- Your auto insurance only covers $500,000
- Your **umbrella policy** pays the remaining $700,000 (plus legal defense costs)

How Much Coverage?

Most attorneys should carry **at least $1–2 million**, with more if:

- You own property or a business
- You have significant investments or savings
- You have young drivers in the household
- You have a public profile or online presence

Umbrella policies are **very affordable**—usually around $200–$500/year per $1 million in coverage.

4. Legal Exposure: Divorce, Lawsuits, and Professional Claims

Even lawyers who are risk-conscious in their careers often overlook personal exposure from life events.

Divorce

- **Prenuptial or postnuptial agreements** are important for protecting premarital assets or business interests
- Keep inheritances separate and avoid co-mingling if you want to

maintain individual ownership
- If you're in a second marriage or blended family, consider using trusts to define inheritance clearly

Lawsuits

- Even outside your law practice, you can be sued—for car accidents, rental property issues, social media activity, or injury on your property
- Keep high-risk assets (rental homes, boats, etc.) owned under LLCs or partnerships
- Don't volunteer personal guarantees unless absolutely necessary

Professional Claims

- Even with malpractice insurance, an attorney might face out-of-pocket costs, reputational damage, or disqualification from certain roles
- Separate your practice's legal risk from your personal finances—especially if you're a solo or small firm partner

5. Keep Business and Personal Finances Separate

If you run your own practice, freelance, or have business ventures on the side, mixing personal and business finances is one of the worst mistakes you can make.

Why It Matters:

- It exposes your personal assets to business creditors and lawsuits
- It can destroy your LLC's or S-Corp's liability protection
- It makes tax reporting messy and opens the door for audits
- It makes valuation and exit planning harder if you ever sell your practice

Checklist for Separation:

- Open a dedicated business checking account
- Pay yourself a regular salary or distribution
- Avoid using business accounts for groceries, gas, or personal expenses
- Save business receipts, track mileage, and log invoices
- File business taxes separately (even if it passes through to your personal return)

6. Be Proactive—Not Reactive

Here's the truth: if you try to shield assets **after** you've been sued or served, it may be too late.

Courts can claw back transfers that look suspicious. That's why the best asset protection happens **before you need it.**

Make it a habit to:

- Review insurance coverage annually
- Update estate plans after life changes
- Reassess titling of major assets (homes, investment accounts, business equity)
- Work with a CPA, estate planner, or asset protection attorney to stay ahead of the game

Final Thoughts: Protect Like a Lawyer—Because You Are One

You already know how fragile legal systems can be. You've helped clients navigate crises, settlements, and courtroom stress. Now it's time to apply that same level of diligence to your own financial life.

Because protecting your personal assets isn't about paranoia—it's about **prudence**.

When you take steps to secure what you've built, you give yourself and your family peace of mind. You create a firewall between your professional risks and your personal future. And you show the same care to your own affairs that you give to your clients every day.

You're not just building wealth. You're building security. And that's worth protecting.

Chapter 13: Estate Planning for Attorneys

Protecting Your Legacy with the Same Precision You Give to Clients

As attorneys, we draft, review, and litigate legal documents every day. We advocate for our clients' futures. We interpret laws, navigate complexity, and protect others from risk. But when it comes to our **own** personal estate planning, many of us delay, defer, or downplay its importance.

Here's the truth: **you need an estate plan—just like everyone else.**

In fact, you may need one more than most.

Attorneys tend to earn more, accumulate assets earlier, and carry a mix of business and personal risk that makes coordinated planning essential. Whether you're just starting your career, in your peak earning years, or planning for retirement, the right estate documents can protect your family, your assets, and your intentions—during life and after it.

Let's break it all down.

1. Why Even Lawyers Need Their Own Estate Plan

It's easy to assume we'll get to it later—or that we already "know enough" to handle things informally. But estate planning isn't about how much you know—it's about what's **in writing**, how it's structured, and how it's **executed** if something unexpected happens.

Without a proper plan:

- Your loved ones may face **confusion, delay, and court involvement**
- Your assets may go through **costly, time-consuming probate**
- Your wishes about medical care, finances, or guardianship may go ignored
- You leave the state—or worse, the courts—to decide what happens next

Even young attorneys without children or significant wealth need basic documents in place.

2. Core Estate Planning Documents Every Attorney Needs

Last Will and Testament

Outlines how your assets are distributed upon death, names guardians for minor children, and appoints an executor.

Without a will, your estate will be distributed by **state intestacy laws**, which often don't reflect your intentions.

Revocable Living Trust

Used to avoid probate, maintain privacy, and streamline the asset transfer process. A revocable trust allows you to:

- Retain control while alive and well
- Avoid court involvement at death or incapacity
- Name successors to manage your assets smoothly

Especially helpful if you:

- Own property in multiple states
- Have children from multiple relationships
- Want to structure distributions (e.g., delay inheritance or protect from creditors)

Durable Power of Attorney (POA)

Allows someone you trust to manage your financial affairs if you become incapacitated. Without a POA, no one—not even your spouse—can access your accounts or make decisions unless appointed by a court.

Health Care Proxy / Medical Power of Attorney

Names someone to make medical decisions if you're unable to. Should be accompanied by a **Living Will** or **Advance Health Directive** that outlines your preferences for end-of-life care.

Beneficiary Designations

Retirement accounts, life insurance policies, and bank accounts with POD/TOD instructions pass **outside of your will**—so make sure your designations are:

- Updated after life events (marriage, divorce, births)
- Aligned with your overall estate plan

3. Special Planning Considerations

Children and Guardianship

If you have minor children, your will should:

- Name **primary and alternate guardians**
- Designate who will manage assets on their behalf (either through a trust or custodianship)
- Outline any instructions around housing, education, or religious upbringing

Second Marriages and Blended Families

Estate planning gets more complex when you've remarried or have children from previous relationships. A trust can:

- Provide for your spouse during their lifetime
- Ensure your children still inherit
- Avoid conflict between surviving spouses and stepchildren

Dependents with Special Needs

If you have a child or adult dependent with special needs, you must avoid disqualifying them from government benefits. A **Special Needs Trust (SNT)** allows you to:

- Provide supplemental support
- Protect eligibility for Medicaid and SSI
- Name a trustee to manage funds long-term

4. Gifting and Minimizing Estate Taxes

While federal estate tax only affects estates above $13.61 million (as of 2024), many attorneys still want to preserve wealth through **strategic gifting**.

Annual Gifting

You can gift up to **$18,000 per person per year** (2024 limit) without filing a gift tax return. Use this to:

- Help children or grandchildren with education or housing
- Reduce your taxable estate over time
- Create legacy gifts while you're alive to witness the impact

Lifetime Gift & Estate Tax Exclusion

Each person has a lifetime exclusion ($13.61 million in 2024). But this is scheduled to **drop in 2026**, making planning more important for high earners.

Charitable Planning

Tools like **donor-advised funds (DAFs)** or **charitable remainder trusts (CRTs)** allow you to:

- Support causes you care about
- Reduce income and estate taxes
- Involve your family in philanthropic decisions

Irrevocable Life Insurance Trusts (ILITs)

Used to remove large life insurance payouts from your taxable estate while providing liquidity for heirs or estate taxes.

5. Coordinate with Your Financial Planner and Estate Attorney

You know this as a lawyer: documents alone aren't enough. They must be **coordinated**, **executed properly**, and **reviewed regularly**.

An estate plan should be developed **in tandem** with:

- Your **financial planner**, to ensure assets are titled properly and aligned with goals
- Your **tax professional**, to avoid unintended consequences or missed opportunities
- A qualified **estate planning attorney**, even if you work in law—because this is one area where objectivity and specialization are critical

Annual or biannual reviews ensure your plan evolves with your life. Major events like marriage, divorce, childbirth, business changes, relocations, or inheritances should always trigger a review.

Final Thoughts: Leave a Legacy, Not a Legal Mess

Estate planning isn't about wealth. It's about intention.

Whether you leave behind $100,000 or $10 million, your plan:

- Makes things easier for your loved ones
- Ensures your voice is heard
- Prevents confusion, conflict, and court involvement
- Reflects your values and priorities

As an attorney, you already understand the power of legal documents. Now use that power to protect the people and causes you care about—before life gives you a reason to regret not planning sooner.

Start with the basics. Build from there. And remember: your legacy isn't just what you leave—it's how well you prepared others to carry it forward.

Chapter 14: Investing Beyond the Basics

Smart Growth Strategies (and Common Pitfalls) for High-Earning Attorneys

By now, you may already be contributing to your 401(k), maxing out your Roth IRA or backdoor Roth, and funding an HSA. Those are the basics—the blocking and tackling of financial security. But for high-income professionals like attorneys, the next step is expanding beyond tax-advantaged retirement accounts.

This chapter introduces you to a wider range of investment opportunities

taxable brokerage accounts, real estate, private deals, and digital assets

while also highlighting the **red flags** that every attorney should be wary of.

Because the higher your income, the more you're seen as a target for bad deals,

scams, and overly complex strategies that promise the world but deliver nothing.

Let's explore how to grow and protect your wealth—without taking unnecessary

risks.

1. Taxable Brokerage Accounts: Flexibility and Liquidity

Once you've maxed out your retirement accounts, the **taxable brokerage account** becomes your next best tool for long-term wealth building.

Why It's Powerful:

- **No contribution limits**
- **No withdrawal penalties**—you can access funds at any time
- Allows for **diversified investing** in stocks, ETFs, index funds, and bonds
- Enables **tax-loss harvesting**, which can offset gains or reduce taxable income

What to Watch:

- You'll owe taxes on:
- **Dividends and interest income** (annually)
- **Capital gains** (when assets are sold at a profit)
- Holding assets for **over 12 months** qualifies you for lower **long-term capital gains** tax rates (0%, 15%, or 20%)

Strategy Tip: Use your brokerage account to save for goals that occur before retirement—like buying a home, launching a business, or funding education for your kids.

2. Real Estate Investing: More Than Just Owning a Home

Real estate can offer income, appreciation, tax benefits, and diversification. But it's not without risk—and it requires more hands-on involvement than buying index funds.

Popular Options for Attorneys:

- **Rental properties**: Single-family homes, condos, or multi-units
- **House hacking**: Living in one unit while renting others
- **Short-term rentals**: Airbnb/VRBO strategies
- **Real estate investment trusts (REITs)**: Publicly traded or private entities that allow you to invest in real estate passively
- **Syndications**: Pooled investments in large deals like apartment complexes or commercial developments

Tax Benefits:

- Depreciation offsets rental income
- 1031 exchanges allow you to defer capital gains when reinvesting in like-kind property
- Mortgage interest and repair costs may be deductible

Risks:

- Market fluctuations
- Tenant issues and vacancies
- Liquidity constraints
- Over-leveraging with debt

Pro Tip: If you're not ready to manage property directly, start with **REITs** or explore **real estate syndications** through reputable platforms or advisors.

3. Private Equity, Syndications, and Passive Income Opportunities

Many attorneys—especially partners or solo practitioners—get approached with private deals. These might include:

- Venture capital
- Private equity funds
- Law firm investments
- Local business partnerships
- Real estate syndications
- Peer-to-peer lending

Why They're Attractive:

- Higher return potential
- Passive income streams
- Portfolio diversification
- Sense of ownership or mission alignment

What You Need to Know:

- **Accredited investor status** is often required (>$200K income or $1M net worth excluding primary home)
- **Illiquidity**: Your money may be tied up for 5–10 years or longer
- **Due diligence is essential**—review financials, management teams, exit plans, and legal docs

Warning: Many attorneys fall victim to "friendly fire" investments—deals pitched by colleagues, clients, or former classmates. Just because someone you know is involved doesn't mean it's safe or smart.

Have your CPA or financial advisor review any private deal **before signing**.

4. Cryptocurrency: Opportunity or Risk?

Cryptocurrency has gained attention as a speculative and sometimes volatile investment class. But should attorneys get involved?

Pros:

- Diversification outside of traditional markets
- High growth potential (in theory)
- Emerging technologies like blockchain may have long-term value

Cons:

- Extreme volatility
- Lack of regulation and investor protection
- Scams, hacks, and tax complexity
- Poor track record of long-term adoption outside of speculation

Strategy Tip: If you're crypto-curious, consider limiting exposure to **1–5% of your investable assets**—an amount you're willing to lose. Treat it like venture capital, not a retirement plan.

Also, understand the **tax implications**:

- Buying and selling crypto triggers capital gains
- Swapping one coin for another is a taxable event
- Payments received in crypto are taxable income

Use tax software or a crypto-savvy CPA to stay compliant.

5. Red Flags and Scams Targeted at High Earners

As your income grows, so does your visibility—and so do the schemes targeting professionals like you. Be cautious of:

Investment Scams:

- **Guaranteed returns**: If it sounds too good to be true, it is
- **High-pressure tactics**: You should never be rushed to invest
- **Unregistered securities or promoters**
- **Overly complex tax shelters** that lack transparency

Insurance Pitch Disguised as Investment:

- Whole life, variable life, or indexed universal life (IUL) products marketed as "retirement strategies" may carry high fees, hidden commissions, and poor returns
- These products may make sense for *some,* but not all—have a **fee-only advisor** evaluate them

Law Firm-Adjacent Risks:

- Investing in a client's business without full disclosure
- Referring clients to investment schemes you haven't vetted
- Signing on as a personal guarantor in a partnership or real estate deal

Final Thoughts: Grow With Clarity, Not Hype

Your money should be working as hard as you do. But it shouldn't be chasing every flashy opportunity or whispered "can't-miss" deal in the hallway.

As you grow your wealth:

- Stay diversified

- Don't invest in what you don't understand
- Get second opinions on every private deal
- Keep your risk aligned with your goals, age, and income needs

And remember—**sophistication doesn't mean complexity**. The most successful attorneys build wealth through steady, diversified strategies, not roulette-wheel investments.

You don't need the next big thing. You need a portfolio that works in real life—not just on paper.

Chapter 15: Preparing for Retirement—Your Next Chapter

Because Life After Law Should Be Your Best Argument Yet

You've spent years—maybe decades—thinking and working like an attorney. But at some point, whether you're 55 or 75, the question changes from "What's my next case?" to "What's next for me?"

Retirement isn't just about numbers in an account. It's about identity, purpose, lifestyle, and freedom. It's about making sure that the next chapter of your life is just as intentional as the career you've built.

This chapter isn't about winding down—it's about planning a *powerful transition*. Whether you want to fully retire, slowly downshift, or pivot into a different kind of impact, we'll help you do it with clarity, confidence, and control.

1. How Much Is Enough? Understanding Retirement Income Planning

One of the biggest questions lawyers ask about retirement is: *"How do I know I'll have enough?"*

That answer isn't just about a magic number—it's about knowing:

- How much you spend now
- How that will change (or not) in retirement
- What income sources will replace your paycheck

- How long your money needs to last

Key Concepts:

- **Replacement Ratio**: Most professionals need 70–85% of their pre-retirement income to maintain their lifestyle, though lawyers may trend higher due to cost of living, travel, or medical needs.
- **Withdrawal Rate**: A common rule of thumb is the "4% rule," meaning you can safely withdraw 4% of your retirement savings per year. But that number can vary based on market conditions and longevity.
- **Sequence of Returns Risk**: Retiring into a market downturn can reduce your portfolio faster than expected—planning asset allocation is critical in the 5 years before and after retirement.

Retirement Income Sources:

- Social Security (timing your benefits matters)
- Pensions (rare, but still exist in some firms/government roles)
- Investment portfolios (IRAs, brokerage accounts, etc.)
- Law firm deferred comp or buyout structures
- Rental property or business income
- Annuities (if used strategically)

Pro Tip: Create a detailed retirement income timeline with a financial advisor. Map out which accounts you'll draw from, when, and how taxes will impact your withdrawals.

2. Retirement Accounts for Attorneys: Firm vs. Solo

If You're at a Firm:

- **401(k) or 403(b)**: Traditional and Roth options may be available
- **Deferred Compensation Plans**: Often offered to partners and senior attorneys
- **Profit-Sharing Plans**: Firm may contribute based on earnings
- **Defined Benefit Plans**: Rare, but some firms still offer these traditional pensions

If You're a Solo or Small Firm Owner:

- **Solo 401(k)**: Allows employee and employer contributions—up to $69,000/year (2024)
- **SEP IRA**: Simpler option, allows up to 25% of compensation
- **Cash Balance Plan**: Advanced strategy that mimics a pension—great for high-income solos
- **Traditional/Roth IRAs**: Use in addition to business retirement plans

Key Planning Points:

- Know your **vesting schedules**
- Review **beneficiary designations**
- Understand **required minimum distributions (RMDs)** after age 73
- Make **catch-up contributions** after age 50 to boost savings

3. Planning Your Transition Out of Full-Time Practice

Retirement from law doesn't have to be a hard stop. In fact, many attorneys prefer a **phased exit**—both for financial and emotional reasons.

Things to Consider:

- Do you want to sell, wind down, or transition your practice?
- Are there junior partners or associates who could buy you out?
- Is there a market for your client base, niche, or firm brand?
- What's your timeline—and what financial runway do you need?

Tactical Steps:

- Notify clients and colleagues early
- Develop a succession or continuity plan
- Work with a valuation expert if selling your practice
- Secure tail coverage for malpractice insurance
- Update your estate plan and business transition documents

Retirement planning isn't just about what you're retiring *from*—it's about what you're building *toward.*

4. Preparing Emotionally (and Mentally) for the End of Your Legal Career

For many attorneys, the idea of retirement is more daunting than exciting—not because they can't afford it, but because they're not sure *who they'll be* without the title, the challenge, or the prestige.

This is normal.

Your identity has been forged in the courtroom, the conference room, the boardroom. You've been the go-to person, the decision-maker, the professional problem solver. Retirement means:

- Losing structure
- Losing recognition
- Losing "busyness"

But it also means **gaining time**, **gaining flexibility**, and **gaining choice**.

Ask Yourself:

- What do I want my days to look like?
- What relationships do I want to invest in?
- What hobbies or passions have I postponed?
- What impact do I still want to make?

Retirement is a blank canvas. Design it, don't drift into it.

5. Phased Retirement: Redefining Work on Your Terms

Many attorneys aren't ready to fully stop working—and the good news is, **you don't have to**. Instead of full retirement, consider a **phase-down strategy** that still provides purpose, structure, and income.

Options Include:

- **Consulting**: Offer expertise to firms or corporations on your own schedule
- **Mediation or Arbitration**: Use your legal background in a lower-stress setting
- **Teaching**: Adjunct professor roles at law schools or universities
- **Board Service**: Many nonprofits and companies value legal experience on their boards
- **Writing, Speaking, or Mentoring**: Give back to the next generation of lawyers

The benefit of phased retirement is that you can continue earning—but on **your terms**. You control your time, your clients, and your pace.

Strategy Tip: Use phased income to delay Social Security, bridge health insurance costs before Medicare, or fund "fun" expenses like travel or hobbies.

Final Thoughts: Retire To Something, Not Just From Something

Retirement doesn't have to mean fading away. For attorneys especially, it can mean:

- A new chapter of impact
- A more intentional use of time
- A better balance between doing and being

But it only works if you plan for it—financially, yes, but also emotionally and professionally.

So whether you're ten years out or two, start asking:

- What legacy do I want to leave?
- What will bring me joy?
- What will keep me healthy, fulfilled, and free?

Because after decades of solving problems for others, it's time to design a future that solves for **you**.

Chapter 16: Investing in Stocks – Where, How, and Why It Matters

Investing in stocks is one of the most effective ways to grow wealth over time. For attorneys, especially those just starting to build their financial foundation, understanding where to invest, how to do it, and why it matters is critical. This chapter offers a clear, no-fluff guide to stock investing—starting with the different types of accounts available and ending with simple, actionable steps to begin.

Why Stocks Matter in Your Wealth-Building Plan

Stocks represent ownership in companies. When you own a stock, you own a small piece of that business. If the business grows and becomes more profitable, the value of your stock increases. Historically, stocks have outperformed nearly every other asset class over the long term, making them ideal for long-term goals like retirement.

For attorneys, whose time is limited and stress levels high, stock investing offers a passive way to build wealth while focusing on your career.

Where to Invest: Choosing the Right Type of Account

Your first step in stock investing is choosing **where** to invest. Here are the most common account types:

1. Roth IRA (Individual Retirement Account)

- **Best for:** Young or mid-career attorneys with moderate income
- **Tax treatment:** Contributions are made with after-tax dollars; investments grow tax-free; withdrawals in retirement are tax-free
- **Contribution limit:** $6,500/year (as of 2025), $7,500 if over age 50
- **Why it matters:** Great for long-term, tax-free growth

2. Traditional IRA

- **Best for:** Attorneys who want a tax break now
- **Tax treatment:** Contributions may be deductible; growth is tax-deferred; taxes paid on withdrawals
- **Contribution limit:** Same as Roth IRA
- **Why it matters:** Useful if you're in a high tax bracket now and expect to be in a lower one later

3. Brokerage Account

- **Best for:** Attorneys who want flexibility and no income or contribution limits
- **Tax treatment:** You pay taxes on dividends and capital gains
- **Why it matters:** Ideal for investing beyond retirement account limits, or for shorter-term financial goals

4. Custodial Account (UGMA/UTMA)

- **Best for:** Parents who want to invest on behalf of their children
- **Tax treatment:** Taxed at the child's rate up to a threshold; then taxed at parent's rate
- **Why it matters:** Long-term wealth transfer and financial education for kids

How to Open an Account

Here's a step-by-step guide to opening your first investment account:

Step 1: Choose a Platform

Pick a reputable and beginner-friendly platform. Some of the best include:

- **Fidelity** – Great customer service, strong research tools
- **Charles Schwab** – Low fees, good for all experience levels
- **Vanguard** – Known for low-cost index funds
- **M1 Finance** – Automated investing and good for those who want to set it and forget it
- **Betterment or Wealthfront** – Robo-advisors that build and manage portfolios for you

Step 2: Decide Which Account to Open

- Want tax-free growth? Start with a Roth IRA
- Want tax savings now? Go with a Traditional IRA
- Want flexibility? Open a brokerage account

Step 3: Fund the Account

- Link your bank account
- Set up automatic transfers (monthly is a great start)
- Start small if needed—even $50/month is progress

Step 4: Choose Your Investments

Most beginner investors should stick with simple, diversified options:

- **Index funds** (e.g., S&P 500 funds)

- **ETFs** (Exchange-Traded Funds that include hundreds of stocks)
- **Target-date retirement funds** (adjust risk as you approach retirement)

Step 5: Stay Consistent

- Set it and forget it
- Reinvest dividends
- Avoid checking it daily
- Increase contributions as your income grows

Tips for Attorney Investors

- **Start now, even if it's small.** Waiting until your salary increases delays your compounding potential.
- **Don't try to time the market.** The best investors invest regularly regardless of market conditions.
- **Diversify.** Don't put all your money in one stock or sector. Use broad index funds.
- **Avoid high-fee products.** Many actively managed funds charge high fees without beating the market.

Why Investing Matters for Attorneys

Your career may come with delayed earnings and student loan debt, but once you start earning, your investing window is wide open. Investing can:

- Build financial independence
- Offer options beyond billable hours
- Allow earlier retirement or semi-retirement
- Help support future law firm launches or sabbaticals

Final Thoughts

Investing in stocks isn't about picking the next Apple or Tesla. It's about building habits that make your money work for you while you work for your clients.

Open the account. Fund it regularly. Let compounding do the heavy lifting.

You don't need to be a financial expert to start. You just need to take the first step.

Part 3: Risk Management and Protection

Building a Fortress Around Your Finances—Before Life Happens

By the time you reach the mid-career stage of your legal journey, you've likely accumulated not just income—but also risk. You may have dependents who rely on you. You might own a home, be growing your investments, or even managing your own practice. Whether you're single or raising a family, your ability to earn and preserve wealth is now central to your financial future.

That's where **risk management** comes in.

Attorneys are in a unique position: you're highly trained, highly paid, and often highly liable. You're not just protecting a paycheck—you're protecting everything that paycheck supports: your lifestyle, your goals, and the people who depend on you.

This chapter is about creating financial protection systems so that a lawsuit, accident, illness, or mistake doesn't destroy everything you've worked for.

Let's walk through the core areas of protection every attorney needs to understand—and act on.

1. Disability Insurance: Protecting Your Income

Your most valuable asset isn't your house or your 401(k). It's your **ability to earn an income**.

If an accident or illness prevents you from practicing law—even temporarily—your bills don't stop. Your loans don't disappear. Your financial plan can't just hit pause.

That's where **disability insurance** comes in.

What to Look For:

- **Own-occupation coverage**: This is critical. It means your policy pays benefits if you can't work in *your specific legal specialty*, even if you could technically work elsewhere.
- **Elimination period**: How long you have to wait after becoming disabled before benefits kick in (typically 60–90 days).
- **Benefit period**: How long you'll receive benefits (commonly until age 65 or retirement).
- **Partial/residual coverage**: Pays if you can work in a reduced capacity and experience income loss.

Pro Tip:

If your firm offers group coverage, that's a good start—but it often isn't portable, and may not be enough. Consider a **supplemental private policy**, especially if your income exceeds $150,000/year.

2. Life Insurance: Covering Your Family's Future

Life insurance isn't for you—it's for the people you'd leave behind.

If someone would suffer financially if you passed away—a spouse, child, aging parent, business partner—you need life insurance.

Two Main Types:

- **Term life insurance**: Simple, affordable, and sufficient for most. Covers you for a fixed term (10–30 years). Pure protection—no investment component.
- **Permanent life insurance (whole, universal, variable)**: More

complex and expensive. Not usually necessary unless used for specific estate planning or business strategies.

How Much Do You Need?

A general rule of thumb is 10–15x your income. But also consider:

- Outstanding debts (including mortgage and loans)
- Children's education
- Spouse's income needs
- Funeral and final expenses

Stick with **term insurance** unless you've had a deep conversation with a fiduciary financial advisor and an insurance-licensed planner about permanent coverage.

3. Health Insurance: Your First Line of Defense

You're likely covered through your employer—but that doesn't mean you shouldn't understand your coverage.

Key terms to know:

- **Premium**: What you pay monthly
- **Deductible**: What you pay out-of-pocket before insurance starts paying
- **Out-of-pocket maximum**: The most you'll pay in a year before full coverage kicks in
- **Copays and coinsurance**: What you pay for services after hitting your deductible

If your employer offers a **High Deductible Health Plan (HDHP)** paired with a **Health Savings Account (HSA)**, take a close look—it's often the most tax-efficient way to save for healthcare and retirement.

Pro Tip:

If you're self-employed, research your state's health insurance marketplace or a professional association plan.

4. Professional Liability Insurance (Malpractice Insurance)

Whether you're in private practice or working in-house, professional liability is a reality of the legal field.

Even the best attorneys can be accused of:

- Missed deadlines
- Conflicts of interest
- Poor client communication
- Errors in legal documents

And even if you didn't do anything wrong, defending a claim can be costly.

Solo and Small Firms:

You need your own coverage. Research reputable carriers that specialize in legal malpractice.

BigLaw and Government Attorneys:

You're often covered under the firm's or agency's umbrella policy. Still, understand the policy limits and exclusions.

Tip:

If you serve on boards, consult, or do pro bono work outside your employer, check if your current coverage extends to those activities.

5. Umbrella Liability Insurance: Extra Coverage for "What If" Scenarios

Umbrella insurance is often overlooked—but for high-income professionals like attorneys, it's essential.

It covers liability **beyond** your home and auto policies. If someone sues you for damages in excess of those limits, umbrella kicks in.

Scenarios where umbrella insurance matters:

- Car accidents with serious injuries
- Someone injured at your home
- Slander or defamation accusations
- Rental property disputes

Coverage Recommendation:

Start with $1 million in coverage. You can often get an additional $1M of umbrella coverage for as little as $150–$300/year.

If you have significant assets, a public profile, or kids driving your car, umbrella insurance is a no-brainer.

6. Estate Planning: The Ultimate Form of Protection

Estate planning isn't just about money. It's about **control, clarity, and compassion**.

What happens if you're incapacitated? Who manages your finances? What if you pass away unexpectedly—does your family know where to find your accounts, passwords, insurance policies?

Core Documents Every Attorney Should Have:

- **Will**: Designates who inherits your assets and who manages the process
- **Durable Power of Attorney**: Gives someone authority to manage your finances if you can't
- **Advance Health Care Directive**: Outlines your medical wishes and appoints someone to make decisions
- **Beneficiary Designations**: Ensure your retirement accounts and insurance policies are up to date

As your assets grow, talk with an estate attorney about **revocable living trusts**, **guardianship**, and **tax-efficient wealth transfer**.

7. Asset Protection for Attorneys

Attorneys can be prime targets for lawsuits—even outside of work.
Protect your wealth by:

- **Keeping personal and business finances separate**
- **Titling assets strategically** (e.g., Tenants by the Entirety for married couples)
- **Avoiding frivolous business partnerships without legal review**
- **Using LLCs for rental properties or side businesses**
- **Maintaining appropriate coverage** for everything you own or owe

Asset protection isn't about paranoia—it's about preparation.

Final Thoughts: Don't Just Build—Protect

It's easy to get excited about investing, growing, and earning more money. And you should. But none of it matters if you haven't built a financial safety net.

Risk management isn't about fear—it's about **freedom**. The freedom to move forward knowing that your family, your career, and your financial future are protected.

The legal profession is demanding enough without adding financial vulnerability to the mix.

Put your defenses in place—then go build your legacy.

Chapter 17: How to Choose Companies to Invest In

Once you've decided to invest in the stock market, the next question is: *where should your money go?* For attorneys—who are often analytical and research-driven—the temptation may be to pick individual stocks based on hunches, headlines, or hype. But smart investing goes beyond speculation. It requires understanding how to evaluate companies and, more importantly, when to keep things simple.

In this chapter, we break down how to research companies, read key financials, understand the basics of stock fundamentals, and explain why index funds are often a more effective choice for long-term investors.

Step 1: Know What You're Investing In

Before investing in a company, ask yourself:

- What does this company do?
- How does it make money?
- Do I believe in its future?

If you don't understand the business model or industry, you probably shouldn't invest in it. As Warren Buffett says, "Never invest in a business you cannot understand."

Step 2: Review Basic Financial Health

Here are the key financial indicators to look for:

1. Revenue (also called "top line")

This tells you how much money the company brings in. You want to see steady or growing revenue year-over-year.

2. Net Income ("bottom line")

This is what's left after all expenses, taxes, and costs. Is the company profitable? Are profits growing?

3. Earnings Per Share (EPS)

EPS = net income divided by number of shares. Higher and growing EPS is usually a good sign.

4. Price-to-Earnings (P/E) Ratio

This compares the company's stock price to its earnings. Lower is not always better, but a very high P/E can signal the stock is overvalued.

5. Debt-to-Equity Ratio

How much debt does the company have compared to shareholder equity? High debt can be risky.

6. Free Cash Flow

Cash left after operating and capital expenses. It's used for dividends, buybacks, and growth.

Step 3: Read the Company's 10-K and 10-Q Reports

These are publicly available filings with the SEC:

- **10-K** = Annual report
- **10-Q** = Quarterly report

They show:

- Business overview
- Financial results
- Risks the company faces
- Management's discussion and analysis

Reading these reports, even briefly, helps you become a more informed investor.

Step 4: Understand Market Trends and Industry Position

- Is the company a leader in its industry?
- How competitive is the market?
- What are the long-term trends (e.g., renewable energy, AI, digital payments)?

Sometimes, even great companies struggle because their industry is shrinking.

Step 5: Evaluate the Management Team

The leadership of a company matters. Look for:

- Experienced, transparent CEOs and boards
- Clear long-term vision
- Low executive turnover
- Shareholder-friendly policies (like buybacks or dividends)

Step 6: Don't Chase Hype

Just because a company is in the news doesn't mean it's a good investment. Hype-driven investing leads to bubbles and poor decisions. Focus on fundamentals, not headlines.

Index Funds: The Smarter Choice for Most Investors

While picking individual stocks is exciting, most attorneys are better off with index funds.

Why Index Funds?

- **Diversification:** Own hundreds of companies with one investment
- **Low cost:** Expense ratios are typically under 0.10%
- **Low maintenance:** No need to track individual stocks
- **Consistent returns:** Match the market, which outperforms most investors over time

Popular Index Funds:

- **S&P 500 Index Funds:** e.g., VFIAX (Vanguard), FXAIX (Fidelity)
- **Total Market Index Funds:** e.g., VTSAX (Vanguard Total Stock Market)

- **International Index Funds:** e.g., VXUS (Vanguard Total International)

How to Decide Between Individual Stocks and Index Funds

Consider Individual Stocks If:

- You enjoy research and analysis
- You understand the business and the industry
- You only invest a small percentage of your portfolio in them

Stick With Index Funds If:

- You want simplicity
- You prefer to spend time on your legal career, not stock analysis
- You want broad exposure and low risk

Final Thoughts

You don't need to be a stock market expert to be a successful investor. Most attorneys are better off focusing their energy on their careers and allowing index funds to quietly build wealth in the background.

If you do invest in individual companies, take the time to understand their business, financials, and future outlook. But always remember: the best portfolio is the one you stick with.

Keep it simple. Stay consistent. Let time and compounding do the rest.

Chapter 18: Financial Planning for Families

Balancing Your Career, Your Loved Ones, and Your Long-Term Vision

Being a lawyer demands time, focus, and energy. When you're also raising a family, supporting aging parents, or coordinating with a spouse or partner, financial planning becomes more than personal—it becomes relational.

You're not just building wealth for yourself. You're making decisions that affect your children's education, your partner's security, your parents' well-being, and the legacy you'll leave behind.

In this chapter, we'll break down how to integrate your legal career with your family goals. Because wealth means little if it doesn't reflect the life you want to build—*together*.

1. Coordinating Finances with Your Spouse or Partner

Whether you both work or one of you manages the home, money conversations are critical to a strong, unified financial life.

Start with Shared Clarity:

- **What are your values?** (Security? Flexibility? Travel? Giving?)
- **What are your short-term and long-term goals?**
- **How do you feel about debt, risk, and spending?**

Approaches to Managing Joint Finances:

- **Full integration**: All income and expenses go into shared accounts
- **Partial integration**: Shared household account + separate personal accounts
- **Fully separate**: Each manages their own income and expenses independently

There's no "right" structure—it's about communication, transparency, and trust. Make sure both partners:

- Know where accounts are and how to access them
- Have visibility into shared expenses and savings
- Are part of key financial decisions (even if one takes the lead)

Action Step: Create a monthly or quarterly "money date" where you review progress, adjust goals, and stay aligned.

2. Planning for Children: Education and Future Security

Raising kids is one of life's most rewarding—and expensive—journeys. From diapers to diplomas, financial planning helps reduce stress and open doors for your children.

Education Savings Tools:

- **529 Plans**: Tax-advantaged savings for education. Funds grow tax-free and can be used for:
- College tuition, fees, books, and housing
- K–12 tuition (limited)
- Student loan repayment (up to $10,000)
- Roth IRA rollover (new option starting in 2024, with limits)
- **UGMA/UTMA Accounts**: Custodial brokerage accounts that become

the child's property at 18 or 21 (depending on state). More flexible than 529s, but less tax-efficient.

- **Roth IRAs for Teens**: If your child earns income (e.g., part-time work), you can contribute to a Roth IRA in their name—setting them up for decades of tax-free growth.

Don't Forget:

- Life insurance (term policies to protect dependents)
- Naming guardians in your will or trust
- Creating a family trust for asset management and protection

Strategy Tip: Start small, start early. Even $100/month into a 529 grows significantly over 15–18 years.

3. Managing Dual-Career Households or Stay-at-Home Spouses

When both partners work demanding jobs—or when one works at home unpaid—financial planning needs to reflect reality, not just income.

For Dual-Career Couples:

- Max out both retirement plans when possible
- Consider filing taxes jointly for most beneficial brackets
- Coordinate benefit elections (health insurance, FSAs, dependent care accounts)
- Be aware of the "marriage penalty" if you're both high earners

For Stay-at-Home Partners:

- Open a **spousal IRA** to help them save for retirement
- Make sure they're covered by **life and disability insurance**, even if they don't earn income (replacement cost of caregiving is significant)
- Ensure estate documents reflect their role in managing assets, guardianship, or health care decisions

Communication is key: Both partners should understand the household's financial picture, even if only one generates income.

4. Caring for Elderly Parents or Family Members

Attorneys are increasingly part of the "sandwich generation"—supporting children while also helping aging parents.

This creates both emotional and financial strain. Planning ahead can ease the burden.

Key Questions to Ask Parents:

- Do you have a will, trust, and power of attorney?
- What are your wishes for health care and end-of-life decisions?
- Do you have long-term care insurance or a plan to pay for care?
- Where are your financial documents and accounts?

Financial Strategies:

- Research Medicaid planning and asset protection options early
- Use a **529A ABLE account** if supporting a family member with disabilities
- Consider a **multigenerational trust** if you'll be caring for both children and parents
- Explore **tax deductions** if you provide more than 50% of a parent's

support

Caring for family is noble—but it shouldn't come at the expense of your own financial security. Set clear boundaries, and get support from financial and legal professionals when needed.

5. Holding a "Family Financial Meeting" and Creating a Legacy Plan

Many lawyers avoid talking openly about money—even with those closest to them. But clarity now prevents conflict later.

Host a Family Financial Meeting:

- Frequency: Once a year or during major life events
- Who: You, your partner, adult children (if appropriate), financial advisor, estate attorney
- Topics:
- Where documents and passwords are stored
- Who is the executor, trustee, or power of attorney
- What values guide your giving or investing
- What your legacy goals are—and how family members are part of that

Create a Legacy Plan:

This goes beyond money. Think about:

- Charitable giving (now or through your estate)
- Family values and stories you want passed down
- Involving your children in philanthropy or business
- Educating the next generation on financial literacy

Your legacy isn't just what you leave—it's what you teach. Give your family the tools to be good stewards of wealth, responsibility, and decision-making.

Final Thoughts: Build Wealth With Your Family, Not Around Them

It's easy to compartmentalize work and home. To grind through the week and hope everything else takes care of itself.

But the most financially successful attorneys aren't just high earners—they're intentional planners. They communicate. They coordinate. And they make sure their financial goals align with the people they love most.

So whether you're newly married, raising kids, supporting your parents, or thinking about your legacy, remember this:

You don't have to do it all alone—but you do have to do it *on purpose*.

Chapter 19: Financial Literacy for the Next Generation

Because True Wealth is Measured in What You Teach, Not Just What You Leave Behind

For most attorneys, success isn't just about earning a high income—it's about using that income to create stability, opportunity, and impact for those you love. But building wealth is only half the story. The other half is preparing the next generation to manage it wisely.

Whether you're raising young kids or supporting adult children, your role as a financial role model is critical. Without guidance, inherited wealth can be squandered, mismanaged, or even become a source of family conflict. With the right education and planning, it becomes a platform for independence, stewardship, and legacy.

This chapter is your roadmap to helping the next generation not just receive wealth—but understand it, respect it, and grow it.

1. Teaching Kids About Money Early

You don't need to wait until your child is in college—or earning their own money—to start financial education. In fact, the earlier you begin, the better.

Age-Appropriate Lessons:

- **Ages 3–7**: Introduce the concept of money as a tool. Use clear jars or envelopes for "spend," "save," and "give." Let them make small purchase decisions and experience trade-offs.
- **Ages 8–12**: Offer allowances tied to effort or chores. Encourage goal-based savings (e.g., a new toy, a gift for a friend). Open a savings account and show how interest works.
- **Teens**: Teach budgeting basics, how to use a debit card, and the dangers of credit. Consider a custodial Roth IRA if they have earned income. Discuss needs vs. wants in real life (e.g., cell phones, cars, clothing).
- **College-Aged or Young Adults**: Introduce tax basics, how to manage student loans, the importance of credit scores, and the magic of compound interest. Consider a matched savings program to incentivize good habits.

Tip: Talk about your own financial journey—including your mistakes. Kids learn more from honest conversations than lectures.

2. Using Wealth to Build Responsibility, Not Entitlement

One of the biggest concerns among high-income professionals is the fear of "ruining" their kids with money. It's a real and valid fear. But the solution isn't to hide money or avoid the topic—it's to shape their mindset.

How to Foster Financial Maturity:

- Emphasize *stewardship*, not ownership. Teach that wealth is a tool to be managed, not flaunted.
- Make giving part of the family culture. Create a giving fund and involve children in choosing causes to support.
- Tie financial privileges to responsibility. Instead of handing over a car, ask them to cover gas or maintenance. Rather than paying for

everything in college, match their part-time earnings.
- Create earning opportunities, not just allowances. Let them work in your office, help with household projects, or tutor siblings to earn money.

Remember: The goal is not to withhold—but to guide.
Your wealth should give your children options—not entitlements.

3. Estate Planning Strategies to Protect Generational Wealth

Once your wealth reaches a certain level, estate planning is no longer just about avoiding probate—it's about preserving values and protecting the next generation from themselves or others.

Common Strategies:

- **Revocable Living Trusts**: Avoid probate, ensure privacy, and allow controlled distributions.
- **Irrevocable Trusts**: Offer greater asset protection and estate tax mitigation. Useful for gifting, legacy giving, or special needs planning.
- **Generation-Skipping Trusts**: Allow wealth to pass directly to grandchildren while skipping a taxable layer.
- **Incentive Trusts**: Distribute funds based on behaviors, achievements, or responsibilities (e.g., graduating college, holding a job, staying sober, giving to charity).
- **Family Limited Partnerships (FLPs)**: Used to manage and transfer business or real estate interests while retaining control.

Consider Also:

- **Naming co-trustees or corporate fiduciaries** for impartial decision-making
- **Life insurance in a trust** to create liquidity for estate taxes or heirs

- **Updating your plan regularly** as laws and family dynamics change

Tip: Be as thoughtful about *how* you leave wealth as you are about *how much* you leave.

4. Encouraging Financial Independence in Adult Children

Your adult children may face very different economic realities than you did—higher housing costs, student loan burdens, and a more volatile job market. It's natural to want to help. But helping shouldn't mean enabling dependency.

Healthy Support Strategies:

- Offer **financial guidance** before financial gifts.
- Set **clear boundaries** and expectations for support.
- Use **one-time gifts** (e.g., down payments, weddings, debt reduction) to empower, not rescue.
- Introduce them to **your financial advisor** or help them find one of their own.
- Consider **graduated inheritances** (e.g., 1/3 at age 30, 1/3 at 35, 1/3 at 40) to allow time for maturity and growth.

Communication Tip: Treat financial conversations with adult children like any other part of parenting—respectful, ongoing, and anchored in love and clarity.

Final Thoughts: Money is a Tool—So Teach Them How to Use It

You've worked hard to earn and grow your wealth. But the most meaningful investment you can make is in the financial education of your children and heirs.

They don't need to be financial experts—but they do need to understand:

- The value of hard work
- The importance of saving and investing early
- How to protect themselves from debt, scams, and poor decisions
- That your legacy is built on principles, not just portfolios

Don't just leave them money. Leave them the **confidence** and **competence** to manage it with purpose.

Because the greatest return on investment comes not from stocks, real estate, or business deals—but from preparing the next generation to carry the torch.

Chapter 20: The Lifestyle You Deserve

Wealth Isn't the Goal—Freedom, Impact, and Joy Are

Lawyers are among the most driven, disciplined, and detail-oriented professionals. You work long hours. You solve high-stakes problems. You hold yourself to impossibly high standards. And when it comes to your finances, that same discipline often means *delayed gratification*. Save more. Spend less. Defer joy. Build the nest egg.

But here's the truth: **wealth is not the endgame**. It's a tool.

You didn't work this hard just to stress over every dollar. You didn't pour your energy into building a career only to feel guilty about enjoying the rewards.

In this final chapter, we're turning the page. You've done the hard work of planning, protecting, and growing your money. Now it's time to think about how that money supports the life you actually want to live.

Let's talk about **joy**, **generosity**, and **freedom**—the lifestyle you've earned, and how to step into it with confidence.

1. Give Yourself Permission to Enjoy Your Wealth

It might sound strange, but many high-achieving attorneys struggle with enjoying their own money. You've spent years being cautious, frugal, strategic—and suddenly, the idea of spending on something just because it brings you joy feels... irresponsible?

It's not.

You Have Permission To:

- Take the vacation without checking your inbox
- Buy the car you want without guilt
- Dine at the restaurant with no mental math
- Hire help at home to reclaim your time
- Treat your family to experiences they'll never forget

The key is **intentionality**, not excess. Enjoying your wealth doesn't mean losing control. It means aligning spending with what matters most to you—comfort, relationships, time, travel, meaning—not just the numbers.

Tip: Budget for joy. Literally. Include a "lifestyle satisfaction" category in your spending plan.

2. Strategic Philanthropy and Charitable Giving

For many attorneys, the next phase of wealth isn't about accumulation—it's about **impact**. Philanthropy allows you to express your values, support your community, and involve your family in a shared mission.

Ways to Give Strategically:

- **Donor-Advised Funds (DAFs)**: Make a tax-deductible gift now and distribute it over time. Great for high-income years or windfalls.
- **Charitable Remainder Trusts (CRTs)**: Provide income to you or your heirs now, with the remainder going to charity later.
- **Family Foundations**: Formalize giving across generations with tax and legacy benefits.
- **Direct Giving**: Sponsor scholarships, community programs, legal aid initiatives, or causes close to your heart.

Why It Matters:

- Charitable giving reduces taxable income
- It teaches children about values, responsibility, and gratitude
- It connects you to something bigger than your practice or paycheck

Reflection: What causes have shaped your life or your legal career? What problems do you feel called to solve? Start there.

3. Use Money as a Tool for Freedom, Peace, and Legacy

The purpose of wealth isn't status. It's **freedom**—the ability to choose how you spend your time, who you serve, what legacy you leave behind.

Freedom means:

- Working because you want to, not because you have to
- Saying no to toxic clients, roles, or obligations
- Taking a sabbatical, switching practice areas, or mentoring full-time
- Spending more time with family, giving back, or just breathing easier

Peace means:

- No longer worrying about bills, emergencies, or the unknown
- Knowing your family is secure no matter what happens
- Having systems in place so you don't manage money every day—it manages itself

Legacy means:

- Passing down more than dollars—passing down *discipline, knowledge, and values*
- Structuring your estate to bless your children without burdening them
- Creating opportunities for others through scholarships, mentorships,

or giving circles
- Documenting your story—not just your accounts—so your impact endures

Financial independence isn't just an idea. It's a tool to live life on your terms.

4. Living Below Your Means While Enjoying Life

There's a common myth that financial literacy means cutting back. In reality, it means **spending well**. You can enjoy a rich lifestyle and still live below your means—if you stay aligned with your values.

Key Principles:

- **Grow the gap**: The bigger the difference between what you earn and what you spend, the faster you build wealth.
- **Avoid lifestyle creep**: Increase savings and investments before upgrading the house, car, or vacation.
- **Automate smart decisions**: Set savings and giving on autopilot so you can enjoy the rest guilt-free.
- **Define success for yourself**: It's not the number of cases, awards, or followers—it's how fulfilled, free, and generous you feel.

Remember: No one ever got to the end of their career and said, "I wish I had spent more time reading financial statements." They say, "I wish I had traveled more, seen my kids more, given more."

Your lifestyle should reflect your *priorities*, not your *position*.

Final Thoughts: You've Built the Life—Now Live It

You've read hundreds of pages. You've thought deeply about budgets, taxes, investments, insurance, legacy, and law firm strategy. You've done the intellectual heavy lifting most people avoid for years.

Now it's time to **live the reward**.

This isn't about permission—it's about perspective. You have one life. You've built wealth not to impress, but to **impact**. Not to hoard, but to **help**. Not to fear the future, but to **step into it boldly**.

So take the trip. Fund the cause. Write the check. Rest more. Stress less. Speak openly about money to your kids, your clients, and your colleagues.

And don't forget—your financial literacy is part of your legacy. Keep learning. Keep growing. And keep living a life you don't need to retire from.

Chapter 21: Financial Literacy and Mental Health for Lawyers

Building Peace of Mind as Well as Net Worth

In a profession known for its pressure, precision, and performance, the last thing most lawyers need is another source of stress. Yet for many attorneys, **money quietly becomes one of the biggest stressors in their lives**—affecting their sleep, their health, their relationships, and even their long-term career choices.

Financial stress doesn't always stem from lack of income. In fact, many lawyers earn well into six figures and still feel financially unwell. The culprit? A combination of high expectations, lack of time, student debt, inconsistent financial education, and the emotional toll of money-related uncertainty.

This chapter explores the critical link between **financial wellness and mental health**—and how financial literacy can be one of the most powerful tools lawyers have to combat burnout and reclaim a sense of control.

1. The Link Between Financial Stress and Burnout in the Legal Profession

Burnout among attorneys is real—and well documented. The causes are familiar: long hours, billable targets, high-stakes cases, demanding clients, and the constant pressure to perform. But layered on top of that is another less visible burden: **financial uncertainty**.

You may be juggling:

- Six-figure student loan debt
- Credit card or lifestyle debt
- The pressure to "look successful" at work and at home
- Unpredictable bonuses or partnership buy-ins
- Tax complexities from 1099 or K-1 income
- Lack of long-term financial planning

And because money isn't something most attorneys are taught to talk about—let alone manage strategically—it often becomes a **silent source of anxiety**.

In studies of mental health in the legal profession, **financial stress is often one of the top contributors to anxiety, depression, and burnout**—especially among early-career and mid-career lawyers.

2. How Financial Anxiety Affects Your Career, Relationships, and Health

When finances feel uncertain or overwhelming, it spills into every area of life.

In Your Career:

- You may **stay in a job you dislike** because you're afraid to leave the paycheck behind.
- You might avoid **going solo or launching a side venture** out of fear of losing financial stability.
- You may **ignore retirement planning** because today's cash flow feels too tight.

In Your Relationships:

- Money is one of the **leading causes of marital tension and divorce**, especially when one partner is "in the dark" about finances.
- You might avoid conversations about budgeting, debt, or long-term goals with your spouse or family.
- You may feel **shame or guilt** about not "having it together" financially, even while earning a strong income.

In Your Health:

- Chronic financial stress is linked to **sleep issues, high blood pressure, digestive problems**, and burnout.
- The constant low-grade anxiety of financial disorganization can sap your energy and focus—making you less effective at work and at home.

The good news? You don't have to be rich to feel financially well. You just need **clarity**, **a system**, and **a shift in mindset**.

3. Creating Financial Routines That Reduce Stress

One of the best ways to lower financial anxiety is to remove uncertainty and disorganization. You can do this by building **simple routines** that keep you proactive, not reactive.

Financial Routines to Reduce Mental Load:

Weekly:

- Review spending (no shame, just awareness)
- Check balances in checking/savings/credit accounts
- Log any irregular income or upcoming expenses

Monthly:

- Pay bills on time (automate where possible)
- Transfer a set amount to savings or investments
- Review credit card balances (and pay them off if possible)
- Revisit progress toward short-term financial goals

Quarterly:

- Review investment performance with your advisor
- Check credit reports (via AnnualCreditReport.com)
- Adjust savings targets or budget based on new goals

Annually:

- Revisit your budget for lifestyle changes
- Rebalance your investment portfolio
- Meet with your financial advisor, CPA, and attorney
- Update beneficiaries and estate documents
- Set one big financial goal for the year ahead

The key: You don't have to check everything every day. Just set a system. The more you automate, the more peace of mind you create.

4. Using Financial Security as a Mental Health Support System

Financial wellness and mental wellness aren't separate—they're interwoven. When you build healthy money habits, you also build:

- **Resilience**: You can weather emergencies without panic.
- **Confidence**: You're making intentional decisions, not reacting to every paycheck.
- **Freedom**: You can say no to toxic clients, say yes to meaningful projects, and protect your time and boundaries.

Financial Security Creates Options:

- The option to take a sabbatical, change practice areas, or downshift into consulting
- The option to prioritize family, health, or passion projects
- The option to retire early or never retire at all—because your choices are yours

Your Emergency Fund = Your Emotional Safety Net

Every lawyer should have a **minimum of 3–6 months' living expenses** saved. It's not just for flat tires or hospital bills—it's for **buying yourself time** when you need it most. That fund can be the reason you leave a toxic job, take a break, or navigate a life transition with peace instead of panic.

Final Thoughts: Mental Wealth is Just as Important as Net Worth

We spend years building our legal knowledge. We take pride in being trusted advisors and sharp thinkers. But too often, we neglect our own well-being—financial and otherwise.

You don't have to carry the anxiety of money management alone.

You don't have to sacrifice mental health to be successful.

You don't have to be perfect—you just have to be intentional.

Financial literacy is **self-care**. It's clarity. It's power. It's a form of protection no one can take from you.

So give yourself permission to slow down. To organize. To ask for help.

And remember: **your greatest asset is not your billable hour—it's your peace of mind.**

Part 4: Long-Term Wealth & Legacy Planning

From Income to Impact—Building a Future That Lasts

As attorneys, you're trained to think ahead—anticipating arguments, reading clauses twice, and seeing the implications of today's decisions far down the road. But when it comes to personal finances, many legal professionals remain locked in short-term thinking: billable hours, bonus cycles, and quarterly tax filings.

It's time to break that cycle.

Long-term wealth and legacy planning is about more than having enough for retirement. It's about aligning your money with your life goals. It's about protecting your family, creating generational opportunity, and having the freedom to choose what comes next—whether that's scaling back, giving back, or transitioning out of full-time practice entirely.

This chapter is about shifting your mindset from **income generation** to **wealth preservation and purpose**—and building a financial life that outlasts your legal career.

1. Defining What Wealth Means to You

Start with this question: *What does wealth mean to me?*

- Is it never worrying about money again?
- Is it owning your time and schedule?

- Is it being able to take a sabbatical, fund a child's education, or support aging parents?
- Is it leaving a legacy behind—financial or otherwise?

Long-term wealth planning begins with clarity. Without a clear definition, you're just chasing numbers. With clarity, your plan becomes personal, purposeful, and more likely to succeed.

2. Your Peak Earning Years Matter Most

For most attorneys, ages 35–55 are your **peak earning years**. This is the season where smart financial moves matter most—because every dollar you save and invest today has time to compound.

Think of these years as the **second half of the game**:

- Your income is likely higher than ever
- You may be reducing debt or building equity
- You still have time to correct earlier missteps or build momentum
- But you also face greater complexity: taxes, family needs, risk exposure, and competing priorities

Your long-term financial strategy should now include:

- **Maximizing retirement contributions** across multiple account types
- **Investing outside of retirement** in brokerage accounts or real estate
- **Diversifying income** through side ventures or passive sources
- **Rebalancing portfolios** annually based on goals and risk tolerance
- **Tax planning** to reduce drag and capture deductions
- **Legacy structures** like trusts, insurance strategies, and giving plans

This is no longer about "getting by." It's about **intentional wealth-building.**

3. Investing with a 20+ Year View

By now, you've likely started investing—but is your strategy aligned with your long-term goals?

Your Plan Should Account For:

- **Asset allocation**: Are you properly diversified across stocks, bonds, real estate, and cash?
- **Time horizon**: Is your risk level appropriate based on how far you are from retirement?
- **Tax efficiency**: Are you using tax-loss harvesting, Roth conversions, or HSA investing?
- **Withdrawal strategy**: Do you know how you'll draw down assets when the time comes?

As your accounts grow, your investing should shift from *just growth* to a balance of **growth, preservation, and income**.

This is where working with a fiduciary financial advisor—ideally one who understands the legal profession—can add real value.

4. Preparing for Life After Law

For many attorneys, retirement doesn't mean stopping altogether. It may mean:

- Transitioning to part-time, teaching, or consulting
- Serving on boards, working in policy, or giving back through pro bono work
- Launching a second career or business
- Relocating to a lower-cost area and living off investments

But **none of that is possible without planning**. You need to run the numbers:

- What's your "enough" number?
- How much will healthcare cost in retirement?
- What income streams will you have?
- When will you draw Social Security or pensions?
- Will your lifestyle and expenses increase, decrease, or stay flat?

A financial plan brings these answers into focus—and turns vague retirement dreams into real, actionable timelines.

5. Estate Planning Is Not Optional

At this stage, your estate plan should be more than just a basic will.
It's about protecting:

- Your assets
- Your loved ones
- Your privacy
- Your wishes

Your Plan Should Include:

- A **revocable living trust** (especially if you own property or want to avoid probate)
- Updated **wills**, **powers of attorney**, and **healthcare directives**
- **Guardianship designations** if you have minor children
- Clear **beneficiary designations** on all retirement accounts and insurance
- A **letter of intent** explaining your values, goals, and instructions for heirs

If you have significant assets or a blended family, consult with an estate attorney who specializes in high-income professionals.

Pro tip: Review your estate plan every 3–5 years or after major life events—marriage, divorce, birth, death, or business changes.

6. Teaching the Next Generation

Wealth without wisdom can do more harm than good. If you have children or dependents, part of legacy planning is **financial education**.

This could include:

- Involving them in family budgeting or investment discussions
- Funding 529 college savings plans
- Creating custodial accounts or trusts with restrictions
- Teaching about budgeting, taxes, and charitable giving
- Sharing family financial history and values

You've worked hard for your money—now make sure the next generation knows how to use it wisely.

7. Charitable Giving and Philanthropy

Legacy isn't just about family—it can also be about impact. Whether you give annually, donate appreciated stock, or create a donor-advised fund (DAF), charitable giving can:

- Support causes you care about
- Reduce your taxable income
- Involve your family in values-based discussions
- Leave a lasting footprint in your community

Talk with your advisor or estate planner about integrating philanthropy into your long-term plan.

8. Write Your Legacy on Purpose

A true legacy isn't about money—it's about meaning. Your legacy includes:

- The wealth you build
- The habits and lessons you model
- The opportunities you create
- The relationships you nurture
- The causes you support

As an attorney, you already shape the lives of clients and colleagues. Now it's time to shape your own financial legacy—by planning, protecting, and living intentionally.

Final Thoughts: Wealth Isn't the Goal—Freedom Is

At this stage of your career, you don't need to hustle harder. You need to think smarter.

You've earned your income. You've grown your assets. Now it's time to **protect, preserve, and pass it on.**

Long-term wealth and legacy planning give you what no hourly rate ever could: freedom. Flexibility. Peace of mind.

Because at the end of the day, your legacy isn't defined by your resume—it's defined by what your money allowed you to build, support, and share.

Make it count.

Chapter 22: Student Loan Nuances Specific to Law School

Smart Strategies for Managing Six-Figure Debt

For many lawyers, **student loans are the first major financial commitment of their adult life**—and one of the most daunting. With law school costs often exceeding $150,000–$250,000, the burden of repayment can shape every financial decision you make in your 20s, 30s, and beyond.

But unlike undergraduates, lawyers often face more complex options—thanks to higher balances, shifting income potential, and special programs designed for those in public service or the private sector.

In this chapter, we'll walk through how attorneys can approach their law school loans with strategy, not stress. We'll break down Public Service Loan Forgiveness (PSLF), when to refinance, how income-driven plans really work, and what you need to know about the tax consequences of forgiveness.

1. Public Service Loan Forgiveness (PSLF): A Lifeline for Public Interest Lawyers

If you work for a **qualifying government or nonprofit organization**, the **PSLF program** could allow you to **have your remaining federal student loan balance forgiven after 120 qualifying payments** (typically 10 years).

Who Qualifies:

- **Public defenders**
- **Prosecutors**
- **Legal aid attorneys**
- **Attorneys at 501(c)(3) nonprofits**
- **Government agencies (local, state, federal)**
- Some roles at public universities and legal advocacy groups

PSLF Requirements:

1. **Work full-time** for a qualifying employer
2. Have **Direct Loans** (or consolidate eligible loans into a Direct Consolidation Loan)
3. Be enrolled in a **qualifying repayment plan** (typically income-driven)
4. Make **120 on-time monthly payments** while meeting the above criteria
5. Submit the **Employment Certification Form (ECF)** annually or when changing jobs

Why It's Powerful:

- Forgiveness is **tax-free** under PSLF
- Enables attorneys to pursue passion-driven work without being financially penalized
- PSLF is especially beneficial for those with **high debt-to-income**

ratios (e.g., $200K+ debt on a $60K–$90K salary)

Caution: PSLF has historically been difficult to navigate due to changing rules, servicer errors, and paperwork issues. **Track everything**. Use the **Federal Student Aid PSLF Help Tool** and keep records of every payment and employment certification.

2. Refinancing vs. Staying in Federal Programs

As your income increases, you'll be tempted to refinance your loans with a private lender—especially when interest rates are high. But for lawyers, refinancing is a **point of no return**—once you do it, you lose access to federal protections like:

- Income-driven repayment plans (IDR)
- PSLF
- Forbearance and deferment options
- Temporary relief programs like CARES Act pauses

When to Consider Refinancing:

- You have a **stable, high income** (e.g., partner-track, BigLaw, in-house)
- You're not eligible for PSLF
- You don't need access to federal hardship protections
- You can get a **lower fixed interest rate** and save significantly over time
- You plan to aggressively pay off loans in 5–7 years

When to Stay in the Federal System:

- You're pursuing **PSLF**
- You might need **income-driven plans** for flexibility
- Your income is still volatile or developing

- You prefer **forgiveness options** after 20–25 years

Pro Tip: Revisit the refinancing conversation **annually**, especially if your income changes. Some attorneys strategically start on IDR, then refinance after a few promotions.

3. Income-Driven Repayment Plans (IDR): Flexibility and Forgiveness

If PSLF isn't right for you—or you're still figuring out your career path—**Income-Driven Repayment Plans (IDR)** can help you manage high debt while keeping your payments tied to income.

Common IDR Plans:

- **PAYE (Pay As You Earn)**: Caps payments at 10% of discretionary income; forgiveness after 20 years
- **REPAYE**: Similar to PAYE but includes interest subsidies; forgiveness after 20–25 years
- **IBR (Income-Based Repayment)**: 10–15% of discretionary income; newer borrowers get 20-year forgiveness
- **SAVE Plan (formerly REPAYE, updated 2023)**: Reduces required payments for low-income borrowers, offers interest forgiveness, and forgives balances faster

Why IDR Can Work for Lawyers:

- You may have **modest early-career income** but large debt
- Payments adjust each year with your income
- Protects you from unaffordable minimum payments in lean years
- Forgiveness (after 20–25 years) is possible—but unlike PSLF, the **forgiven amount is taxable**

What You Need to Know:

- You must **recertify income and family size** annually
- Payments are based on **AGI** (Adjusted Gross Income), which can be lowered through deductions (like 401(k) or HSA contributions)
- The longer you stay in IDR, the **more interest may accumulate**

Planning Tip: If you plan to stick with IDR for long-term forgiveness, you must also plan for the "**tax bomb**"—the IRS will treat forgiven debt as income.

4. Tax Implications of Forgiven Loan Balances

This is one of the most misunderstood aspects of federal student loans: **not all forgiveness is tax-free**.

PSLF = Tax-Free Forgiveness

If you qualify for Public Service Loan Forgiveness, you will owe **no federal income taxes** on the forgiven amount. This makes PSLF arguably the most generous loan program available.

IDR Forgiveness (20–25 Years) = Taxable

If you receive forgiveness through an IDR plan (not PSLF), the balance forgiven is treated as **ordinary taxable income** in the year it's forgiven.

Example:

If you have $150,000 forgiven after 25 years, that $150,000 will be **added to your taxable income**—possibly resulting in a $40,000+ tax bill, depending on your tax bracket.

Planning for the Tax Bomb:

- Build a **"forgiveness sinking fund"** to cover future taxes
- Invest separately in a taxable account to prepare
- Consider timing forgiveness with a **low-income year** (e.g., after retirement, career change)

Note: As of the **American Rescue Plan Act of 2021**, all federal student loan forgiveness is tax-free through **2025**. Whether this continues depends on future legislation.

Final Thoughts: Make Your Student Loan Plan Work for You

Student loans are a tool—not a trap. But they require **strategy, clarity, and consistency**. Whether you're a public interest attorney, a solo practitioner, or climbing the BigLaw ladder, your path will look different—but it should always be intentional.

Here's a recap of how to approach your loan decisions:

- **If you're in public service**, certify for PSLF immediately and make sure you're on an IDR plan.
- **If you're unsure about your path**, stay in federal programs until your career stabilizes.
- **If your income is high and stable**, consider refinancing to save on interest and pay off loans faster.
- **If you're on IDR for the long haul**, plan now for the tax burden—and be ready to celebrate when that day comes.

In the end, your law school loans are just one part of your broader financial picture. With smart planning, you can move from feeling trapped by debt to feeling empowered by your strategy.

Chapter 23: Financial Planning for BigLaw vs. Boutique vs. Government vs. Solo Practice

Because Your Financial Plan Should Match Your Career Track, Not Someone Else's

Every legal career is different—but money touches all of them. Whether you're billing 2,200 hours in a glass tower, advocating for underserved communities, building your own firm, or carving out a niche in a boutique practice, your financial plan should reflect your income, lifestyle, values, and long-term goals.

The problem? Law school didn't teach you how to align money with your career path. Too many lawyers enter the workforce with six-figure debt, unclear compensation structures, and pressure to "keep up" financially—without a clear understanding of what it takes to build wealth sustainably in their chosen setting.

This chapter breaks down how to financially plan for four major legal career paths: **BigLaw, boutique firms, government/public interest, and solo practice.** Each path has its pros, challenges, and strategic considerations. There's no "best" route—only what works for you.

1. Income Differences and Expectations

BigLaw

- **Starting salary (2024):** $215,000+
- **Bonuses:** $15,000–$100,000+ depending on year/class and hours
- **Growth potential:** $500K–$1M+ as partner
- **Tradeoff:** Long hours, high stress, limited time to manage your money

Boutique Firm

- **Starting salary:** $75,000–$140,000+
- **Bonuses:** Often smaller but can be profit-sharing or discretionary
- **Growth:** Steady, with earlier client contact and partner potential
- **Tradeoff:** Less prestige, but better work-life balance for many

Government/Public Interest

- **Starting salary:** $55,000–$85,000
- **Bonuses:** Rare or small (retention bonuses, bar passage bonuses)
- **Benefits:** Strong retirement plans, health insurance, and PSLF eligibility
- **Tradeoff:** Modest income, but financial stability and mission-driven work

Solo Practice / Small Firm Owner

- **Income:** Varies dramatically ($0–$500K+) depending on niche, clients, and marketing
- **Bonuses:** You write your own—based on net revenue
- **Flexibility:** High, but requires business skills
- **Tradeoff:** High risk/reward, inconsistent income early on

2. Bonus Structures and How They Vary

Bonuses can shape cash flow, taxes, and savings—but they're not created equally across practice types.

BigLaw Bonuses

- Typically **year-end or semiannual**
- Often tied to **billable hour thresholds**
- Can be **substantial**—but highly **taxed**, often 35%+ withholdings
- Should not be relied on for essential expenses

Planning Tip: Save or invest bonuses immediately. Use them to fund emergency reserves, retirement, or debt payoff—not lifestyle upgrades.

Boutique & Government Bonuses

- More likely to be **modest or project-based**
- May include **holiday bonuses**, **bar passage bonuses**, or **longevity incentives**
- Less predictable, but usually stable once earned

Solo Practitioner Income

- No formal bonuses—but the ability to **scale revenue** through strategic pricing, client acquisition, and niche marketing
- "Bonuses" are reinvestments, owner draws, or profit-sharing with staff

3. The Lifestyle Creep Trap in BigLaw

High salaries don't always lead to financial freedom—especially if your expenses rise with your income.

Many BigLaw associates fall into **lifestyle inflation**:

- Luxury apartments
- Designer wardrobes
- Lavish vacations
- Constant food delivery and Uber rides
- Outsourcing everything to save time

While some of these are time-saving investments, others are **emotional spending** to cope with burnout.

How to Avoid It:

- **Treat your base salary like your "real" income**, and save your bonus
- **Automate 20–30% of income** into retirement and brokerage accounts
- **Delay large upgrades** (cars, homes, watches) until your savings rate is on track
- **Track spending** to stay self-aware—not guilty

Wealth isn't about what you earn—it's about what you keep and grow.

4. Budgeting on a Modest Government or Public Interest Salary

Government lawyers often make less—but many are more financially secure over time due to **lower expenses**, **stable benefits**, and **student loan forgiveness**.

Smart Strategies:

- Use **income-driven repayment** and **PSLF** to eliminate law school loans
- Maximize **government pension systems** and 457(b)/403(b) accounts
- Budget based on **net income**, not gross
- Share expenses with roommates or spouses early in your career

- Delay large financial decisions (e.g., homeownership) until your career and income stabilize

Note: If your salary is under $90K and you have $150K+ in federal loans, PSLF is almost always the better path than aggressive payoff.

5. Building Wealth Without a BigLaw Income

You don't need a $215K salary to become financially independent—you just need **consistency, intentionality, and time**.

Steps Every Lawyer Can Take:

- **Live below your means**, even if your peers don't
- **Automate savings**: 15–20% of income into retirement accounts
- Use **Roth IRAs, HSAs, and 401(k)/403(b)** options
- Start a **low-fee brokerage account** for long-term investments
- **Avoid lifestyle traps**: expensive homes, luxury cars, eating out daily
- Build **passive income**: rental property, writing, speaking, teaching, or a legal blog

Remember:

- A $90K salary with a 25% savings rate can outperform a $300K salary with a 0% savings rate
- Financial freedom is about **habits, not headlines**

Final Thoughts: Align Your Money With Your Mission

Every legal career path offers different challenges and opportunities—but the financial fundamentals don't change:

- Spend less than you earn

- Save and invest consistently
- Avoid lifestyle creep
- Plan with your future self in mind

Don't compare your income to others—compare your **savings rate**, your **peace of mind**, and your **alignment with what matters**.

Whether you're in BigLaw or building your own path, the key to long-term success is the same: **intentional financial planning that supports your career, your family, and your life beyond the law.**

Chapter 24: Time Management and Delegating Financial Tasks

How Busy Lawyers Can Build Wealth Without Adding More to Their Plate

Lawyers are some of the most time-strapped professionals in the workforce. Between billable hour quotas, client emergencies, administrative work, and firm obligations, there often isn't much mental bandwidth left to organize finances, review investment accounts, or even pay bills on time.

That's why it's crucial to treat **time as a currency**—and to create systems that reduce your cognitive load, not increase it. The good news? With the right structure, financial wellness doesn't have to be time-consuming. In fact, once automated or delegated properly, it often requires less than an hour a month to stay on track.

This chapter is about building a **systematic financial life** that supports your long-term goals while respecting your limited time. We'll explore what to automate, what to outsource, and how to make smart financial decisions with minimal friction.

1. Lawyers Are Time-Poor—But That Doesn't Excuse Avoidance

If you're like many attorneys, you probably delay financial tasks because they feel time-consuming, tedious, or low on the priority list. But here's the reality: **ignoring your finances costs you more time and money down the line.**

Without a plan, you may:

- Miss payments or get hit with late fees
- Forget to contribute to retirement accounts
- Let investment opportunities pass you by
- Delay tax prep until April 14th (or beyond)
- Stay in a financial fog that leads to stress and poor decisions

A proactive system solves this. **You don't need more time—you need more structure.**

2. Automate What You Can

Automation is the easiest way to ensure consistency with minimal effort. Once set up, it works in the background, freeing you to focus on your clients and your life.

Key Areas to Automate:

1. Bill Payments

- Set up automatic payments for recurring bills (mortgage, rent, utilities, student loans)
- Use calendar reminders for quarterly tax estimates or credit card due dates
- Use a dedicated checking account for monthly bills only (for better

visibility)

2. Savings Contributions

- Automate monthly transfers to emergency savings
- Set rules like "save 10% of every deposit" via banking tools
- Split direct deposits to send a portion straight into savings

3. Retirement Contributions

- Contribute a fixed percentage to your 401(k), 403(b), or SEP IRA
- Schedule monthly contributions to a Roth IRA or brokerage account
- Rebalance your portfolio automatically (most custodians allow this)

4. Credit Card Payments

- Set to auto-pay in full each month to avoid interest
- Review your statements once a month to track spending

5. Investing

- Use robo-advisors or target-date funds that automatically manage allocations
- Set up recurring contributions, not one-off deposits

Bonus: Use apps like **Mint, Monarch, Rocket Money**, or **YNAB** to automate expense tracking and budgeting.

3. Delegate What You Shouldn't Be Doing Alone

Being a great attorney doesn't make you a great financial manager. And that's okay. Delegation isn't a weakness—it's a strategy.

When to Outsource:

1. Financial Advisor

- You want help creating a plan for retirement, taxes, investments, or cash flow
- You're unsure how to structure your finances for goals like buying a home or exiting the profession
- You're busy and want a professional to monitor everything
- Ideal if you're a high-income earner but not confident in DIY investing

2. CPA or Tax Professional

- You have complex income (W-2 + K-1, 1099s, or law firm distributions)
- You need help with tax planning, not just filing
- You do side work (consulting, writing, real estate)
- You're worried about underpaying or misfiling
- You want a professional to coordinate with your advisor or estate attorney

3. Bookkeeper or Virtual Assistant

- You run your own firm or practice
- You're tracking multiple income sources or business expenses
- You want help reconciling accounts, categorizing deductions, or handling admin

4. Estate Planning Attorney

- You have dependents or own a business
- You want to protect assets, assign guardians, and minimize taxes
- You need help structuring trusts, charitable plans, or succession

4. Time as a Currency: The ROI of Hiring Professionals

It's tempting to DIY everything to save money—but remember, your time has value. And if you bill at $300/hour but spend five hours doing taxes, you just gave up $1,500 of billable time to avoid paying a CPA $600.

The right professionals don't just save you time—they:

- Help you avoid costly mistakes
- Save you money through better tax planning and investment strategy
- Provide peace of mind and reduce mental fatigue
- Help you stay compliant, organized, and proactive

Ask Yourself:

- What tasks cause me the most financial stress or confusion?
- What is the cost (in time and money) of continuing to delay or DIY?
- What would it be worth to have this handled well and consistently?

Think of professionals as your financial team—there to help you make informed decisions and stay on course.

5. Build Your "Financial Operating System"

Here's a simple framework to organize your financial life around time-efficiency:

CategorySystem/ToolAction

Income Tracking

Pay stubs, law firm distributions

Review monthly; confirm deductions

Budgeting

Mint / YNAB / spreadsheet

Automate categorization & savings

Bill Pay

Bank autopay or credit card auto-pay
Confirm due dates; pay in full monthly
Saving
Auto-transfer to savings/investment accounts
Set rules based on % of income
Investing
401(k), IRA, brokerage with auto-invest
Rebalance annually or use robo-tools
Tax Planning
CPA or quarterly reminders
Schedule Q1–Q4 payments and prep early
Estate Docs
Estate planning attorney
Review every 3–5 years

Final Thoughts: Do Less—But Do It Smarter

You don't need to be a financial expert to build a strong financial future. But you do need to respect your time, your stress level, and your limits.

Automation and delegation are **not shortcuts—they're strategy**.

So free yourself from the daily financial grind. Build a system that runs quietly in the background. Assemble a team that helps you do your best thinking for others while protecting yourself.

Because in the end, **time is your most valuable asset.** Spend it wisely.

Chapter 25: Evaluating Equity in a Legal or Business Setting

Understanding Ownership, Opportunity, and the Hidden Fine Print

At some point in your legal career, you may be offered more than just a paycheck. Whether it's **equity in your law firm**, a **slice of ownership in a startup client**, or a **compensation structure tied to shares**, it's a turning point—and a major financial decision.

Equity can be one of the most powerful tools for building long-term wealth—but it can also be **a trap** if you don't understand the terms, risks, and implications.

In this chapter, we'll walk through how to evaluate equity offers, including law firm partnerships, startup shares, and alternatives like phantom equity. You'll learn when it makes sense to trade salary for ownership—and when it's better to take the check and keep walking.

1. What Is Equity—and Why It Matters

Equity represents **ownership**. It means you have a stake in the entity's value—and in its success (or failure).

In legal and business settings, equity can come in various forms:

- **Partnership shares** in a law firm
- **Stock options** or **restricted stock units (RSUs)** in a startup or corporation

- **Phantom equity** or **profit-sharing** (ownership without actual shares)
- **Equity buy-in opportunities** at boutique firms, consultancies, or alternative legal services platforms

The appeal is obvious: If the company grows, your equity becomes a valuable asset. But with that potential comes complexity—and risk.

2. When Equity Comes Into Play

Here's where you're likely to encounter equity opportunities as an attorney:

Law Firm Partnership:

- Equity partners share in profits and governance of the firm.
- Often requires a **buy-in**, either lump-sum or over time.
- Profit shares may fluctuate, and capital contributions may not be liquid.
- In some firms, equity partners also take on **liability** (especially in small or general partnerships).

Startup or Corporate Client:

- Offered in exchange for legal services or early contributions.
- Equity may be in the form of **stock options**, **RSUs**, or **founder shares**.
- Often illiquid, speculative, and subject to **vesting** and **exit scenarios**.
- May require balancing conflict-of-interest rules and bar ethics guidelines.

Internal Business Ventures:

- If you're helping launch a new practice group, side venture, or legal tech company, you may be offered **sweat equity**.
- Phantom equity or profit pools are more common in firms hesitant to give formal shares.

3. How to Evaluate Equity-Based Compensation Offers

Before you say yes to equity, ask yourself and the offering party the following:

Key Questions:

- What **type of equity** is being offered? (Actual shares, options, RSUs, phantom equity?)
- What **percentage of the company** or firm does it represent?
- What is the **valuation** of the entity—and who determined it?
- Are there any **restrictions on selling** or transferring the equity?
- What are the **terms of vesting**? (When and how does your ownership become real?)
- What **events trigger a payout** or liquidity event? (Acquisition, IPO, retirement?)
- Are there **tax implications** upon grant, vesting, or sale?

You also need to compare the equity offer to traditional compensation:

- Are you giving up base salary or guaranteed bonus in exchange for equity?
- How long will it take before this equity becomes financially meaningful?
- Are you assuming **more risk or workload** without a guaranteed reward?

4. Understanding Dilution, Vesting, and Phantom Equity

Let's break down a few important terms every attorney should know when reviewing an equity offer:

Dilution

Occurs when more shares are issued—reducing the percentage of ownership each shareholder has.

Example: If you own 5% of a startup and new investors come in, your stake might shrink to 3% unless protected.

Vesting

Refers to how much of the equity you "own" over time.

Example: A 4-year vesting schedule with a 1-year cliff means you don't own any equity until you've been with the firm for a year. After that, you gain rights to a portion monthly or annually.

Phantom Equity

You don't get actual ownership, but you receive cash or bonuses as if you did—based on the company's performance or value. Often used when employers want to share profits without giving up control.

Buy-In / Capital Contribution

In many law firms, equity partnership requires you to "buy into" the firm—this can range from $25,000 to $500,000+. You may need to finance this or negotiate terms.

Exit Rights / Buyback Clauses

What happens if you leave? Does the company or firm buy your equity back? At what valuation? Is it fair?

5. When to Say Yes (or No) to Equity Instead of Salary

Equity can be a smart wealth-building tool, but it shouldn't come at the cost of **financial stability or clarity**.

Say Yes to Equity When:

- You're passionate about the venture and have **long-term alignment** with its mission
- You can afford to wait for the potential payout (5–10+ years)
- You have confidence in the management, business model, and exit plan
- The equity is **in addition to** a strong base salary or other benefits
- You're being **fairly compensated** for your contribution

Be Cautious or Say No When:

- The equity replaces most or all of your salary
- There's no clear **path to liquidity** or value realization
- You're assuming substantial **risk, hours, or liability** without upside
- The valuation is inflated, or the ownership stake is unclear
- You need cash now and can't afford to speculate

Remember: Equity is not cash. You can't pay your mortgage with shares in a company that doesn't yet have revenue.

Final Thoughts: Equity Is a Financial and Legal Decision

As an attorney, you're trained to spot risk, understand contracts, and negotiate terms. Use that training to advocate for yourself—especially when equity is on the table.

Equity offers can create **life-changing wealth**, but only if:

- The structure is fair

- The business is sound
- The terms are clear
- The role is aligned with your goals

Don't be afraid to bring in your own **financial advisor or attorney** to evaluate the deal. And don't let the excitement of "ownership" override the need for due diligence.

Because when it comes to equity, you're not just working for a paycheck—you're investing your time, energy, and reputation.

Make sure the return is worth it.

Chapter 26: Charitable Giving and Philanthropic Strategy

Giving Back with Purpose, Tax Savvy, and Long-Term Vision

As a high-income professional, you may reach a point in your career where your financial priorities shift. You've paid off loans, built savings, and are planning for retirement. Now, you're ready to **make a meaningful impact**—not just through your practice, but through charitable giving.

Philanthropy isn't just about writing checks. For attorneys, it can be a way to express values, create a legacy, reduce taxes, and involve your family in something bigger than billable hours.

This chapter explores how to give strategically—whether in your peak earning years, during transitions, or as part of your estate. We'll cover tax-smart strategies, donor-advised funds, appreciated stock donations, and long-term legacy planning through trusts, foundations, and endowments.

1. Structuring Giving for High-Income Years

The most effective giving happens **intentionally**—when your generosity is aligned with your tax strategy and financial goals. If you're in your highest-earning years (e.g., partnership, in-house counsel, law firm owner), smart giving can reduce taxable income **and** support causes you care about.

Why Give Strategically:

- High earners may face **federal tax rates of 35–37%**
- Charitable donations are tax-deductible if you itemize
- Giving in high-income years reduces current taxes **and supports future plans**

How to Structure Your Giving:

- **Bunch donations** into high-income years to exceed the standard deduction
- Coordinate giving with **year-end bonuses, windfalls, or capital gains events**
- Use tools like **donor-advised funds (DAFs)** to spread gifts over time while claiming full deductions now

2. Using Donor-Advised Funds (DAFs)

DAFs are one of the most powerful and flexible tools for charitable giving—especially for attorneys with fluctuating income or those looking to give over time.

What is a DAF?

A **donor-advised fund** is like a charitable investment account. You contribute to the fund now (and get an immediate tax deduction), then recommend grants to charities over months or years.

Why DAFs Work for Lawyers:

- **Immediate deduction** even if you grant funds later
- **Invested funds grow tax-free**, increasing your charitable impact
- **No need to manage private foundations or file separate returns**

- Great tool to involve children or partners in **family philanthropy**

How to Use a DAF:

1. Open one through a sponsor (e.g., Fidelity Charitable, Schwab Charitable, Vanguard, or a community foundation)
2. Contribute cash, stock, or even real estate
3. Invest the assets for potential growth
4. Recommend grants to IRS-qualified charities anytime

Pro tip: Use a DAF to give big in high-income years (e.g., sale of firm equity, bonuses, etc.) while preserving control over when and where you distribute.

3. Giving Appreciated Stock vs. Cash

One of the smartest strategies for high-income attorneys is to **donate appreciated assets instead of cash**.

Why It's Powerful:

- You **avoid capital gains tax** on the appreciation
- You get a **charitable deduction for the full fair market value**
- It preserves your cash flow

Example:

You bought stock for $5,000 that's now worth $25,000.

- If you sell it, you'll pay capital gains tax on $20,000
- If you donate it directly, you pay no tax—and deduct the full $25,000

Assets You Can Donate:

- Publicly traded stock
- Mutual funds or ETFs
- Real estate
- Private business interests (with proper planning)
- Crypto (to some nonprofits)

How to Do It:

- Work with your financial advisor or custodian to transfer shares directly to the nonprofit or into a DAF
- Ensure the charity can accept non-cash assets
- Keep good records for IRS reporting

4. Legacy Giving Through Trusts, Foundations, or Endowments

If your goal is to create a long-term impact—even after your lifetime—consider **legacy philanthropy**. These strategies not only reduce estate taxes but also preserve your values for future generations.

A. Charitable Trusts

- **Charitable Remainder Trust (CRT):** You (or your heirs) receive income from the trust now; the remainder goes to charity later. Great for reducing taxes on appreciated assets.
- **Charitable Lead Trust (CLT):** The charity receives income now; your heirs get what's left after a set period. Ideal for estate tax reduction and multigenerational planning.

B. Private Foundations

- A more hands-on vehicle than a DAF, foundations allow you to:
- Hire staff
- Set giving priorities
- Control investment strategy
- Requires setup, annual IRS filings, and ongoing management
- Best for families giving **$1M+ over time** or who want governance and control

C. Endowments

- Create a **permanent giving vehicle** at a university, nonprofit, or community foundation
- Can be named in your honor or a family name
- Typically requires a minimum gift (e.g., $25,000–$100,000)
- Supports causes like scholarships, legal aid, public service fellowships, etc.

5. Involving Your Family and Firm in Your Giving

Giving is more powerful when it's collaborative. Use your philanthropy to:

- Teach children about values and money
- Bring your spouse or partner into shared decision-making
- Inspire colleagues to contribute to causes through pro bono, firm matching, or shared funds
- Establish scholarships for future lawyers or underserved communities

Questions to Consider:

- What causes shaped your life or legal journey?
- What legacy do you want to leave outside your career?
- How can you use your wealth, experience, and name to lift others?

Final Thoughts: Give With Intention, Not Just Impulse

Charitable giving isn't just a tax strategy—it's a life strategy. When done thoughtfully, it becomes one of the most fulfilling uses of your wealth and your story.

You've worked hard to build success. Now you have the chance to build **significance**.

Whether you give $5,000 or $500,000, whether it's through a DAF or a scholarship, the point is to **be intentional**—and to give in a way that aligns with your values, your goals, and your long-term vision.

Because real wealth isn't just about what you accumulate—it's about what you share.

Chapter 27: Transitioning Careers or Retiring Early

Financial Freedom Isn't Just for the Ultra-Wealthy—It's for Lawyers, Too

Many attorneys spend years climbing the legal ladder—only to look up and ask, "Is this it?" For some, the work becomes draining. For others, passions evolve. For many, burnout becomes too loud to ignore.

Whether you dream of retiring early, taking a sabbatical, pivoting into teaching or consulting, or simply scaling back, the truth is this: **You need a plan.**

This chapter explores how lawyers can financially prepare for career transitions, early retirement, or lifestyle downshifts—without sacrificing their long-term financial health or identity. We'll also dive into the FIRE movement (Financial Independence, Retire Early) and how attorneys can apply it on their own terms.

1. Planning for Burnout, Sabbaticals, or Mid-Career Shifts

Burnout in the legal profession is real—and rising. If you're experiencing it now, or you've seen it coming, you're not alone.

Common Warning Signs:

- Chronic fatigue, even after weekends
- Cynicism toward clients, colleagues, or your work
- Diminished performance despite long hours
- A growing urge to "escape" or do something else

But burnout doesn't always require quitting. It may mean a **strategic pause**, such as:

- A 6–12 month **sabbatical**
- A shift into **public service, academia, or nonprofit work**
- Moving from **full-time to part-time or of counsel**
- Starting a **second career** in coaching, business, or policy

Financial Preparation Tips:

- Build a **12-month emergency or "career gap" fund**
- Practice **living on less** now to increase flexibility later
- Run the numbers: What do you really need each month to live well but lean?
- Consider **health insurance options** if leaving your firm (COBRA, ACA, spouse plan)
- Create a **career transition budget** with room for retraining, travel, or relocation

Remember: You don't need to wait for total burnout to plan a smarter career rhythm.

2. Financial Independence and the FIRE Movement for Attorneys

The **FIRE movement**—Financial Independence, Retire Early—is a lifestyle and planning philosophy focused on maximizing savings, reducing unnecessary spending, and investing early to reach a point where work becomes **optional**.

It's gaining traction among lawyers—especially those disillusioned with 60-hour weeks and minimal freedom.

Key FIRE Concepts:

- Save **50–70% of your income** in early years (yes, really)
- Invest in **low-cost index funds**, real estate, or business assets
- Achieve "**lean FIRE**" (minimal lifestyle), "**barista FIRE**" (part-time work), or "**fat FIRE**" (comfortable, luxury retirement)

How Lawyers Can Apply FIRE:

- Use **high BigLaw income** to stockpile investments in your 20s and 30s
- Keep lifestyle inflation in check—even when making six figures
- Max out all retirement accounts early: 401(k), HSA, Roth IRA
- Invest in **taxable brokerage accounts** for flexible access before age 59½
- Calculate your "**FI number**" (typically 25x your annual spending)

You don't have to retire at 40 to benefit from FIRE principles. Many lawyers aim for semi-retirement by 50, consulting roles, or scaling down to meaningful part-time work.

3. Preparing for an Exit Strategy (Even If You're Not Retiring Soon)

Exit planning isn't just for partners or private firm owners. Every attorney should have a plan for how they'll **step back**, **transition**, or **leave law altogether**—on their own terms.

Why You Need an Exit Plan:

- Life can change quickly (illness, burnout, family needs)
- Opportunities arise unexpectedly (judgeships, teaching, board work)
- You may want to **leave while you're ahead**—not when you're forced out

Steps to Create an Exit Strategy:

1. **Define your "enough" number**: What would it take for you to walk away confidently?
2. **Diversify your income**: Build passive streams so your salary isn't your only source
3. **Document your clients, systems, and key relationships** for transition or sale
4. **Plan benefits coverage** (health, disability, life insurance) post-employment
5. **Talk with your spouse or family** about your ideal timeline and goals
6. **Build a legacy plan**: What do you want to be known for after law?

Whether it's 3 years or 30 years away, exit planning gives you power and peace of mind.

4. How to Scale Back Without Sacrificing Income or Quality of Life

You don't have to go from full-speed to full stop. Many attorneys now choose to **scale back**—reducing hours, changing practice areas, or taking consulting roles—without cutting income drastically.

Options for Scaling Back:

- Go **of counsel** to your current firm or a boutique
- Transition to **contract work, mediation, or compliance** roles
- Join a **virtual law firm** with flexibility and lower billables
- Take on **teaching**, **CLEs**, or **coaching new lawyers**
- Create **info products, courses, or writing income** on the side

Financial Tips to Make It Work:

- **Downsize debt** before scaling back
- **Refinance high-interest loans** (e.g., private law school debt)
- Reduce fixed costs: housing, car, insurance, subscriptions
- Use **health savings accounts (HSAs)** and **taxable accounts** for pre-retirement access
- Make retirement contributions while you can—**don't pause investing**

You don't have to choose between peace and prosperity. With good planning, you can have both.

Final Thoughts: Freedom is the Ultimate Goal

You became a lawyer to make a difference, solve problems, and live a good life. But that life doesn't have to look like 60-hour weeks until age 65.

Whether you're burning out or simply planning ahead, remember this: **Financial independence gives you options.** It lets you walk away from what no longer serves you—and walk toward a career or lifestyle that feels aligned, healthy, and fulfilling.

Retiring early isn't about quitting—it's about choosing.

Transitioning doesn't mean failure—it means **evolution**.

So if you're dreaming of change, start planning today. Build your cushion. Diversify your income. Protect your energy. And get clear about what "enough" really looks like.

Because at the end of the day, the goal isn't just to bill more hours—it's to live a life you don't need a vacation from.

Chapter 28: Stupid Investments – Schemes That Trap Attorneys

Introduction: When Smart People Make Dumb Money Moves

Attorneys are some of the sharpest, most detail-oriented professionals in the world. You've spent years mastering case law, building arguments, and protecting your clients' interests. But when it comes to managing your own money, even the smartest lawyers can fall for financial traps that cost them big.

This chapter is about those traps—the investments that look exciting on the surface but often lead to regret. Whether it's a buddy's startup, a slick real estate deal, or a too-good-to-be-true crypto scheme, we're going to unpack why attorneys fall for these pitches, what red flags to watch for, and how to protect your wealth the same way you'd protect a client: with strategy, caution, and evidence.

Why Lawyers Fall for Bad Investments

- **High Earning Potential, Low Financial Training:** Your income can rise quickly, but financial literacy often lags behind.
- **Busy Schedules, Outsourced Decisions:** Long hours and packed calendars mean you may trust others to make money decisions for you.
- **Colleague Influence:** If a senior partner is doing it, it must be legit, right?
- **Delayed Gratification Mentality:** After years of schooling, student loans, and low-paid clerkships, there's a desire to catch up—and

sometimes that means overreaching.

- **Status Pressure:** You're surrounded by peers who drive nice cars, take luxury vacations, and invest in shiny ventures.

Common Investment Traps and How to Spot Them

1. **"Exclusive" Private Investments** You get pitched an early investment in a startup, app, tech platform, or real estate venture. It's exclusive, urgent, and supposedly low-risk.

- There's no audited financials.
- No one can clearly explain how it makes money.
- You're told to act fast.

Reality: The majority of early-stage startups fail. Most private investments are high-risk and illiquid.

1. **Overhyped Real Estate Syndications** You're invited to invest in an apartment complex or office building with promises of passive income and tax benefits.

- The operator isn't well known.
- You don't understand the fee structure.
- Returns are presented as guaranteed.

Reality: Many syndications underperform—or worse, aren't properly vetted. Know the team, the plan, and the terms.

1. **Ponzi Schemes and "Passive Income Machines"** You're pitched a trading bot, crypto miner, or forex fund that delivers consistent monthly returns.

- You're told others (including lawyers) are getting paid.

- The system is complicated or vague.
- You're encouraged to bring in friends or colleagues.

Reality: If you don't know how the money is made, it's probably made from new investors—i.e., a Ponzi scheme.

1. **Restaurant and Bar Investments** Your college roommate wants to open a wine bar downtown, and you're invited to be a "silent partner."

- You're emotionally attached to the concept.
- There's no proven operator or business plan.

Reality: Most restaurants fail. These ventures are often passion projects, not profit machines.

1. **MLMs in Disguise** You're approached to sell premium teas, supplements, or tech gadgets through a "business in a box" that rewards recruiting others.

- High buy-in required.
- Success is tied to building a team under you.

Reality: MLMs usually benefit those at the top. Professionals often lose money and credibility.

1. **Unregulated Legal Tech or Finance Startups** You hear about a litigation funding startup or legal software tool that's going to revolutionize the industry.

- No users, no traction.
- The founders lack legal or business experience.
- The tech is untested or unnecessary.

Reality: Many of these ventures burn out before ever gaining real traction.

Why Smart Lawyers Make Dumb Money Moves

- **Overconfidence Bias:** You're used to being the smartest person in the room.
- **Herd Mentality:** You follow what colleagues are doing—without vetting.
- **Anchoring Bias:** "I make six figures, I can afford to lose $20K."
- **FOMO:** You don't want to miss out—even if you don't understand the opportunity.

Ask These Questions Before You Invest

- Do I fully understand the investment?
- What's the worst-case scenario?
- Is this money I can afford to lose?
- Has the investment been reviewed by an independent financial advisor or attorney?
- Am I making this decision based on facts or feelings?

Smarter Wealth-Building Alternatives

- **Low-Cost Index Funds and ETFs:** Reliable, diversified, and low-fee.
- **Backdoor Roth IRA Contributions:** Especially useful for high-income earners.
- **Taxable Investment Accounts:** Great for flexibility and long-term growth.
- **Real Estate (Well-Researched):** Rental properties or REITs can provide steady income.
- **Paying Off High-Interest Debt:** Risk-free, guaranteed return.
- **Investing in Your Skills:** Courses, certifications, and leadership programs can boost income and career satisfaction.

Case Studies

- **Attorney B and the Boutique Fund:** Invested $60,000 into a hedge fund operated by a college friend. It folded within two years. No returns.
- **Attorney L and the Long Game:** Maxed out 401(k), contributed to a Roth IRA, and built a conservative ETF portfolio. After six years, he grew his net worth by $500,000.
- **Attorney M and the Lounge Fail:** Invested $75,000 into a cigar bar project. Never turned a profit. It closed after 14 months.

Red Flags That Should Stop You Cold

- Pressure to act fast
- Promised guaranteed returns
- Unclear or missing financial documentation
- Friends or colleagues involved who lack experience
- Fear-based or hype-based language

How to Say No—Without Burning Bridges "Thanks for thinking of me. I have a very structured investment plan and only move forward after professional review. I hope your venture does well."

Final Thought: It's Not About Being Flashy—It's About Being Free The smartest investors aren't the flashiest. They don't chase hype, they don't follow crowds, and they don't treat investing like gambling. They play the long game.

As an attorney, you already know how to spot weaknesses, assess risk, and protect others. It's time to do the same with your wealth.

Be boring. Be consistent. Be free.

Chapter 29: Helping Without Hurting – How to Support Loved Ones Without Going Broke

How to Set Boundaries With Family and Friends When You're the First to "Make It"

Let's talk about one of the most difficult, emotional parts of becoming a lawyer and earning a high income—especially if you're the first in your family to do so.

You've worked hard. You've sacrificed years of your life, taken on massive student debt, and endured grueling hours that most people wouldn't survive. Now that you're finally earning real money... you're expected to share it.

Help your mom who raised you solo? Of course. Support your dad who worked two jobs and always showed up? It feels like the least you can do. Bail out a cousin, sibling, or friend who says, "You're a lawyer now—you got it"? You want to say yes. You don't want to seem cold. You feel responsible.

But if you're not careful, you'll spend the prime of your earning years putting out everyone else's fires—while your own financial foundation stays on shaky ground.

This chapter is about love—with limits. Support—with structure. Generosity—without guilt. Because your job isn't to fund everyone else's life. Your job is to build a life—and a legacy—that lasts.

You Are Not the Family's Retirement Plan

When you're the first one to "make it," people look to you. Some will ask directly. Others will expect it silently.

You are not a bottomless pit of money. You are not a bank. You are not the family pension.

Even if you choose to help, it must be structured, intentional, and limited. If you let guilt write the checks, your future will bounce.

The Monthly Support Budget Strategy

Let's say you want to help on a regular basis—with rent, groceries, tuition, or emergencies.

Decide what you can give *without* sacrificing your goals.

Example: You decide $1,000/month is your limit.

- $500 goes to your mother's rent
- $300 helps a sibling with tuition
- $200 is on a prepaid card for incidentals

Once you hit $1,000, you stop. When someone else calls?

You say: "I've hit my support budget this month. Let's talk again next month."

That's not harsh. That's healthy. That's not selfish. That's smart.

The One-Time Gift Strategy

Maybe you want to give—but only once. That's fine too.

Example: You receive a bonus and choose to give your parents $5,000 to pay down debt.

You say: "This is a one-time gift. I'm glad to help in a meaningful way, but I can't give more after this."

No reloads. No monthly handouts. Just love—with limits.

What If Everyone Needs Help?

Then set a total budget for the year—say, $12,000—and divide it however you want.

Example:

- Mom gets $500/month
- Dad gets $300/month
- Sibling gets $100/month

- Longtime friend gets $100/month

That's $1,000/month—and you're done.

No one gets more because their story is more emotional. You're generous, but not reckless.

Say It Early. Say It Clearly.

If you don't say anything, people assume your wallet is wide open. That makes "no" feel like betrayal later.

Instead, set the tone: "I'm proud to be in a position to help, but I have boundaries. I've created a monthly/annual support budget. Once I hit it, that's it."

When someone says, "But just this once…" You say: "I love you, but I'm sticking to my plan. I have to protect my future too."

Signs You're Enabling, Not Helping

- They've stopped trying to fix things on their own
- They expect your help
- They guilt-trip you when you say no
- You're solving the same problem over and over
- You feel resentment, not peace

To Avoid This:

- Pay bills directly—don't give cash
- Offer resources, not just money
- Make help temporary, not open-ended
- Don't loan what you can't afford to lose
- Set boundaries: no loans, no IOUs, no guilt

If someone's asking every month? They don't need a check. They need a financial plan.

If They Get Upset, Let Them

They might say: "You've changed." "You forgot where you came from."

"You think you're better than us."

Let them.

Because you didn't go through law school, bar exams, clerkships, and billable hour burnout just to be your family's personal ATM.

Let them be mad. Let them adjust. One day, when they see you financially stable and still standing strong, they'll understand.

Final Thoughts: Give With a Plan—Not Pressure

You're not heartless for saying no. You're not selfish for protecting what you worked for. You're not wrong for building boundaries.

You can still give. You can still love. You can still honor your roots.

But do it:

- With clarity
- With structure
- With peace
- With purpose

The best thing you can give isn't just a check. It's an example—of discipline, planning, and long-term thinking.

That's how you shift your family's future. That's how you change the narrative. That's legacy.

Chapter 30: How to Start Investing

Don't Just Earn It—Build Something With It

You finally made it. After years of training, exams, late-night shifts, and loan deferments, you're earning real money. Whether it's your first law firm paycheck, a signing bonus, a partnership draw, or a contingency case payout, the urge to celebrate is real.

New car? Weekend getaway? Maybe even a home upgrade? All valid. But the real flex?

- Financial independence.
- Long-term wealth.
- Getting your money to work as hard as you do.

That's what investing is about. And the sooner you start, the sooner you buy back your time, freedom, and peace of mind. This chapter is your playbook: how to start investing, which accounts make sense for attorneys, and how to build a plan that turns income into wealth—whether you're earning $100K, $300K, or scaling toward seven figures.

Step 1: Understand What Investing Actually Is

Investing means putting your money into assets—stocks, bonds, ETFs, real estate—that grow in value over time and may generate income.

Instead of letting your earnings sit in a checking account (or vanish on Amazon and Uber Eats), you're giving that money a job. It works 24/7 to build future wealth.

It's not about chasing "hot tips" or picking the next Tesla. It's about consistency and compound growth.

The earlier you start, the more your money can multiply—especially when reinvested over decades.

Step 2: Know Your Goals and Time Frame

Ask yourself:

- When will I need this money?
- Am I okay with short-term market fluctuations?
- Am I investing for retirement, lifestyle upgrades, or business expansion?

If you won't need the money for at least 5–10 years, investing it is usually a wise move. But if it's for a down payment, tuition, or an emergency fund, keep it in cash or low-risk accounts.

Pro Tip: You can—and should—invest while paying off student loans. Just don't use short-term money for long-term goals.

Step 3: Choose Your Investment Accounts

Not all investment accounts are created equal. Some have tax advantages, some have restrictions, and others offer flexibility.

Here's a breakdown tailored for attorneys:

Roth IRA

- Funded with after-tax dollars
- Grows tax-free
- Withdrawals in retirement are tax-free
- 2025 contribution limit: $6,500
- Must have earned income and fall under the income limit

Why it's great: Attorneys early in their career (especially in public interest law or lower tax brackets) can lock in long-term tax-free growth.

Traditional IRA

- Contributions may be tax-deductible
- Grows tax-deferred

- Pay taxes when you withdraw in retirement
- Same $6,500 limit

Best for: Attorneys who want a tax break now. Deductions phase out if you also have a workplace plan.

Taxable Brokerage Account

- No contribution limits or income restrictions
- Taxes on dividends and capital gains
- Full flexibility

Best for: High earners who've maxed out tax-advantaged accounts. Also great for wealth building outside retirement.

401(k), 403(b), or 457 Plans

- Employer-sponsored plans
- 2025 employee contribution limit: $23,000
- Employer match (if available) is extra
- Pre-tax or Roth options

Best for: Law firm associates and partners with access to workplace retirement plans. Take full advantage, especially if there's a match.

SEP IRA

- For self-employed attorneys (solo firms, contract lawyers, consultants)
- Contribution limit: 25% of compensation, up to $66,000 (2025)

Best for: Solo practitioners or side hustlers.

Solo 401(k)

- For self-employed attorneys with no employees
- Higher contribution limit than Roth/Traditional IRAs

Best for: Lawyers running their own firm, contract attorneys, or those consulting on the side.

Step 4: What to Do With a $100,000 Windfall

Whether it's a bonus, inheritance, settlement payout, or consulting success—here's how to turn $100K into long-term momentum.

Step 1: Set Aside Taxes If this is non-W-2 income (like freelance writing, legal consulting, or expert witness work), set aside 30–40% for taxes.

$100,000 × 30% = $30,000 Put this in a separate account. Do not touch it.

Step 2: Fund Your Roth IRA Assuming you qualify (or via a backdoor Roth), contribute the max: $6,500 into a Roth IRA Invest it in a diversified stock index fund (like the S&P 500).

Step 3: Invest in a Taxable Brokerage Account Put $35,000–$45,000 into a brokerage account Pick low-cost ETFs or index funds. Keep it simple and long-term.

Step 4: Establish an Emergency Fund Set aside $10,000–$15,000 in a high-yield savings account for unexpected expenses (case costs, firm expenses, family emergencies).

Step 5: Enjoy a Little Allocate $5,000–$10,000 for a vacation, personal splurge, or treat. Just make it intentional.

Recap: How a Lawyer Breaks Down $100K

- $30,000 – taxes
- $6,500 – Roth IRA
- $35,000 – brokerage investments
- $15,000 – emergency savings
- $8,500 – discretionary spending

This is how attorneys turn income into wealth.

Step 5: Set It and Stick With It

No $100K bonus? No problem. Apply the same principles monthly:

- Save for taxes
- Max out retirement accounts

- Build your cash cushion
- Invest consistently
- Spend intentionally

Automate contributions. Choose simple funds. Avoid overthinking.

Because real wealth isn't built overnight—it's built with smart, consistent actions repeated over time.

Final Thoughts: Don't Let a High Income Be a Missed Opportunity

Earning well doesn't guarantee wealth. You probably know lawyers who earn $300K+ and are still living paycheck to paycheck. You also know lawyers who invest $2,000/month, drive modest cars, and are financially free before 50.

The difference isn't income—it's intention.

Start now. Even $100/month makes a difference. Let your money work while you bill hours. Let it grow while you practice law. Let it create the freedom your profession won't always give you.

Because the real win isn't just making a good living—it's building a great life.

Part 5: Family, Lifestyle, and the Big Picture

Designing a Financial Life That Serves More Than Just Your Career

You became a lawyer for a reason. Maybe it was to help people. Maybe it was for the challenge. Maybe it was for the prestige, the paycheck, or the opportunity to write your own future. Whatever your "why," at some point, your career became more than just a job—it became your identity.

And while you've likely poured years of energy, intellect, and time into your profession, this chapter asks a bigger question: *Is your financial life serving your whole life—or just your work life?*

Too many attorneys get stuck in a loop: more hours, more money, more stress. They chase promotions, bonuses, and milestones without asking whether those achievements are creating the lifestyle they actually want.

This section is your permission—and your blueprint—to step back, look at the big picture, and make sure your money is helping you live a life that feels as good on the inside as it looks on paper.

1. What Do You Want Your Life to Actually Look Like?

This isn't a trick question. But it is one most people never stop to answer.

If you're married, raising children, or supporting aging parents, your income supports more than just your own needs. It becomes a tool for safety, opportunity, and stability. But it should also support **joy**, **growth**, and **time together**.

Ask yourself:

- How many hours per week do I want to work?
- How many vacations do I want to take?
- Do I want to live in a high-cost area, or am I open to relocating?
- Do I want to fund private school, college, or support family members?
- When do I want to scale back, retire, or pivot careers?

These aren't "retirement" questions—they're **lifestyle design** questions. And your answers will shape how you budget, invest, and plan from this point forward.

2. Aligning Money with Family Values

If you have a partner, kids, or close family members who rely on you, finances aren't just about spreadsheets. They're about communication and clarity.

That means:

- Setting joint goals with your spouse or partner
- Having clear, regular conversations about spending, saving, and giving
- Making space for differing financial styles—and meeting in the middle
- Assigning financial roles (e.g., who pays bills, who manages investments, who tracks expenses)

Pro Tip: Hold a "family finance night" quarterly or annually to:

- Review budgets and goals
- Update account access and insurance info
- Check in on savings progress
- Make big-picture decisions together

Money affects relationships more than almost anything else. Transparency now prevents tension later.

3. Raising Financially Literate Children

Your kids are watching how you handle money. Whether they're five or fifteen, they're learning from your habits—good or bad.

Ways to teach without lecturing:

- Talk openly about saving and spending decisions
- Let kids help with grocery lists and budget limits
- Open savings accounts for allowance or birthday money
- Match their savings (e.g., 1:1 for every dollar they save)
- Involve them in charitable giving decisions

If they're older, walk them through:

- How credit cards work
- How to create a budget
- What student loans actually cost
- The basics of investing (compound interest, Roth IRAs)

Legacy isn't just about leaving money—it's about leaving **understanding**.

4. Supporting Family Without Overextending

Many attorneys feel pressure to support others—financially and emotionally. Whether it's helping a sibling, aging parents, or grown children, generosity is admirable—but it has to be sustainable.

Ask yourself:

- Can I afford to give this gift without sacrificing my own financial goals?
- Is this a one-time need or an ongoing pattern?

- Would it be better to offer support in non-financial ways (time, connections, education)?
- Do I need to set boundaries with love and clarity?

Consider creating a "family fund"—a separate savings account earmarked for helping others. This lets you give from a place of structure, not guilt.

5. Lifestyle Inflation: The Quiet Threat

As your income grows, so do your opportunities—and your temptations.

You upgrade your home, your car, your wardrobe, your travel. And suddenly, a six-figure salary doesn't feel abundant—it feels necessary.

This is **lifestyle inflation**, and it's one of the biggest threats to building wealth.

Counter it by:

- Increasing your savings and investment rate with every raise
- Automating wealth-building before lifestyle upgrades
- Keeping fixed costs (housing, car, subscriptions) in check
- Prioritizing spending on experiences and time—not just things

You don't have to live like a broke student forever—but make sure your lifestyle grows *after* your net worth does.

6. Relocation, Work Flexibility, and Quality of Life

If the pandemic taught us anything, it's that location and work flexibility matter more than we thought.

Ask yourself:

- Do I want to live near extended family?
- Am I willing to move to reduce cost of living?
- Would I trade income for time, freedom, or peace of mind?

As an attorney, you may have more flexibility than you think:

- Remote or hybrid legal work
- Moving in-house to reduce hours
- Opening your own firm on your terms
- Teaching, consulting, or pivoting part-time

The law can be all-consuming—but only if you let it be. Your financial stability gives you the power to redefine your career around your life, not the other way around.

7. Your Money Should Reflect Your Priorities

If someone looked at your spending over the last 90 days, would they know what matters most to you?

- Are you investing in your health?
- Are you prioritizing time with loved ones?
- Are you supporting causes that align with your values?
- Are you building a buffer to protect your future?

Money is just a magnifier. It amplifies what you already value. Make sure your budget, savings, and investments reflect who you are—not just what society says you should pursue.

Final Thoughts: Big Picture > Bigger Paycheck

You've worked hard for everything you've earned. And yes, the income matters. But your real wealth isn't measured in your W-2 or your 401(k).

It's measured in time, peace, options, freedom, and legacy.

Financial literacy isn't just about numbers—it's about alignment. About using money as a tool to build the life you want, with the people you love, doing the things that matter.

You don't need to be perfect. You just need to be intentional.

Your future is waiting—and you get to design it.

Chapter 31: Beyond the Billable Hour – Side Hustles and Income Streams for Attorneys

Chapter Title: Beyond the Billable Hour: Why Every Attorney Should Build Multiple Streams of Income

Most lawyers are taught to think of income as linear: bill the hours, earn the check, repeat. But this one-dimensional approach is risky. A layoff, health issue, burnout, or economic downturn can derail your income—and the average law firm doesn't offer much of a safety net.

That's why more and more attorneys are pursuing income diversification—creating alternative revenue streams outside of their primary legal practice. Whether it's teaching a course, investing in real estate, or launching a side business, these streams not only provide financial cushion but often create more autonomy, creativity, and long-term wealth.

This chapter explores the why and how of income diversification for attorneys—and offers practical strategies for adding new streams while staying compliant with professional and ethical boundaries.

Why Income Diversification Matters

Even high-earning lawyers face financial instability if they rely on a single source of income. Diversification helps:

- Reduce risk from layoffs, client loss, or market downturns
- Protect income if you reduce hours, go part-time, or transition careers
- Unlock freedom to say no to clients or cases that don't align with your

values

- Create passive or semi-passive cash flow beyond billable hours
- Build assets and legacy for retirement or generational wealth

The goal isn't to juggle ten jobs—it's to build a few streams that work quietly in the background while you focus on your primary role.

Proven Income Streams for Attorneys

1. Teaching

- Adjunct roles at law schools or undergrad institutions
- CLE course development or bar review instruction
- Online courses via platforms like Teachable, Kajabi, or Udemy

Why it works: You leverage your expertise to educate others, create recurring revenue, and boost your professional brand.

Compliance Tip: Check with your firm if you plan to teach outside the firm's scope or use firm-branded materials.

2. Writing or Publishing

- Authoring legal guides, how-to books, or practice management content
- Monetizing a blog, Substack, or legal newsletter
- Ghostwriting for legal publications or business sites
- Writing children's books, fiction, or non-legal works

Why it works: Writing builds visibility and thought leadership. Self-publishing or licensing rights can generate passive income.

Compliance Tip: Avoid disclosing client details or confidential firm processes. Use disclaimers when discussing legal content.

3. Real Estate

- Owning rental properties (residential or commercial)
- Passive investing in REITs or real estate syndications
- Short-term rentals or Airbnb

- Real estate flipping (for hands-on investors)

Why it works: Real estate offers appreciation, tax advantages, and ongoing cash flow—especially appealing for high earners.

Compliance Tip: Keep investment activities completely separate from your law firm practice, especially if clients are involved in real estate.

4. Board Service

- Paid board roles at nonprofits, startups, banks, or educational institutions
- Equity-based compensation for early-stage or advisory board positions
- Speaking and fundraising roles

Why it works: You get compensated for your strategic insight—not your time—and often receive equity or honoraria.

Compliance Tip: Disclose potential conflicts and document boundaries if board service intersects with firm clients or industries.

5. Consulting and Side Businesses

- Legal consulting for firms, government agencies, or businesses
- Practice area coaching or mentorship for new attorneys
- Starting a business (legal tech, e-commerce, speaking, coaching)

Why it works: You monetize your skills in ways that don't require a J.D.—and create income streams that can scale beyond hourly work.

Compliance Tip: Review bar rules on advertising, referrals, and dual roles. Create clear boundaries between your law practice and your business.

Legal and Ethical Considerations

You're not just a professional—you're a licensed one. Which means any business or side income needs to comply with state bar ethics rules, particularly around:

- Conflicts of interest

- Unauthorized practice of law
- Use of legal knowledge for business gain
- Advertising and disclosures

How to Stay Compliant:

- Use separate LLCs or business entities for any non-law business
- Maintain separate email, bank accounts, websites, and branding
- Avoid giving legal advice in business ventures unless clearly identified as legal services
- Consult your state bar or ethics counsel if unsure
- Disclose dual roles to clients when relevant

How to Legally Separate Business Income from Law Firm Work

It's critical to avoid blurred lines—especially if you're a partner, associate, or of counsel at a firm.

Best Practices:

- Form a separate entity: Create an LLC, S-Corp, or sole proprietorship for the side venture
- Use separate accounts: Open a business bank account for all side income
- Create contracts: Outline roles and scope clearly in writing especially for consulting
- Check your employment agreement: Some firms restrict external income or require disclosure
- Maintain separate time logs: Don't track non-law activities as billable hours or use firm time/resources

Example: If you create a CLE course, make sure:

- It's hosted on your own platform (or a third-party site)
- You don't use your law firm logo, name, or clients as examples
- You disclose any affiliations or disclaim legal advice

Final Thoughts: Build Streams That Support Your Freedom

You went to law school for a reason—but you're more than your license. You have ideas, passions, and the capacity to create wealth in ways that don't rely on hourly billing.

Whether you start a real estate portfolio, launch an online course, or invest in a consulting business, you're creating resilience, options, and long-term impact.

Because true wealth isn't just about net worth—it's about freedom. And multiple income streams buy you choices, stability, and peace of mind.

Chapter 32: Designing a Life, Not Just a Legal Career

For many attorneys, success is measured by billable hours, titles, and the prestige of their firm or clients. But too often, that narrow definition leads to burnout, disillusionment, or waking up one day wondering, "Is this all there is?"

This chapter is about something deeper: shifting your mindset from building *just* a legal career to building a life. A life you actually want to live. One that balances ambition with meaning, finances with freedom, and purpose with progress.

The Problem with Traditional Legal Metrics

From law school onward, most attorneys are trained to:

- Maximize hours billed
- Climb the firm ladder
- Chase partnership or high-profile roles

But this tunnel vision can lead to:

- Chronic stress and anxiety
- Burnout and health issues
- A disconnect from personal goals or family life

When your only scoreboard is the billable hour, you risk losing sight of your real values.

Redefining Success

True success means:

- Having time for your family and passions
- Feeling energized by your work
- Building financial independence that gives you options
- Knowing you're living in alignment with your values

The good news? You don't have to give up your career to live this way. You just have to plan with purpose.

Purpose-Driven Planning vs. Passive Career Drift

Too many attorneys drift through their careers:

- Taking jobs because they "look good"
- Saying yes to everything to avoid disappointing others
- Prioritizing what the firm values over what they value

Purpose-driven planning means:

- Setting personal and professional goals *before* chasing titles
- Creating a financial plan that aligns with your desired lifestyle
- Saying no to things that don't serve your bigger picture

Designing Your Ideal Life: A Framework

1. Identify Your Core Values

Ask yourself:

- What kind of person do I want to be?
- What do I want my days to look like?
- What matters more than money to me?

2. Create a Lifestyle Vision

This includes:

- Where you want to live
- How much time you want to spend working
- What kind of work you find meaningful
- Who you want to spend your time with

3. Build a Financial Roadmap to Support That Vision

- Budget with your goals in mind (not just income targets)
- Save and invest with timelines (early retirement? part-time work?)
- Consider geographic arbitrage or remote work if flexibility is key

4. Set Boundaries to Protect That Vision

- Limit hours
- Reduce toxic clients
- Advocate for flexibility

5. Periodically Reassess

Your values and goals will evolve. Make time each year to check in:

- Are you living the life you envisioned?
- What needs to change?

Practical Financial Moves to Buy Back Time

- **Invest early and consistently** to let compound interest do the heavy lifting
- **Pay off debt strategically** to reduce financial pressure
- **Use your legal knowledge** to create alternative income (writing, teaching, consulting)
- **Save aggressively** in your 30s and 40s to allow options later
- **Automate your finances** so you're building wealth even when life gets busy

Examples of Purpose-Driven Attorneys

- A litigator who transitioned to part-time work and spends three days a week with his kids
- An in-house counsel who teaches a law school course on Fridays and finds joy in mentoring
- A BigLaw associate who built an online course for young lawyers and earns passive income
- A public interest attorney who moved to a lower cost-of-living area and paid off her loans fast

Final Thoughts

Your legal career is a chapter. But your life is the book.

Don't just build a resume—build a life. One that reflects who you are, what you care about, and where you want to go. Because financial freedom isn't about "quitting" the law. It's about being free *within* it—to work how you want, live how you choose, and thrive on your own terms.

Design your life with the same intention and care that you bring to your legal work. That's how you win—at the office and beyond.

Chapter 33: Legacy Planning – Teaching Your Values, Not Just Leaving Your Valuables

Legacy planning isn't just about transferring assets. It's about transferring wisdom. The most meaningful legacies go beyond money—they reflect the values, beliefs, and principles you want to pass down to your family and community.

In this chapter, we'll explore how attorneys can craft a legacy that includes not just what you *leave behind,* but *what you stand for.*

What Is Legacy Planning?

Legacy planning is the combination of:

- Financial and estate planning
- Family education
- Charitable and philanthropic strategies
- Intentional value transfer

It's about designing a future that reflects your life's work and purpose.

Why Legacy Planning Matters for Attorneys

As attorneys, we're often involved in the estate planning process for others—but don't always create a clear roadmap for our own families. We may accumulate wealth, titles, and influence, but without a legacy plan, much of that can be lost or misused.

A thoughtful legacy plan:

- Preserves family wealth and harmony
- Provides for your heirs in meaningful ways
- Prepares your children or beneficiaries to manage what they inherit
- Reinforces the values that guided your life

Core Components of a Legacy Plan

1. A Clear and Updated Estate Plan

- Wills, trusts, powers of attorney
- Beneficiary designations on accounts
- Tax-efficient strategies for high-net-worth families

2. A Family Mission Statement

Outline your values and the principles that matter most:

- What does money mean to our family?
- How do we define generosity, success, and responsibility?
- What causes or communities do we want to impact?

3. Education Around Wealth and Responsibility

Equip your children or heirs with the tools they need to be responsible stewards:

- Financial literacy education
- Conversations about budgeting, investing, and philanthropy
- Modeling decision-making and discipline

4. Ethical Wills and Letters

An ethical will isn't a legal document, but a personal one. It shares your stories, hopes, and guiding principles:

- Life lessons
- Family history
- Spiritual or philosophical beliefs

These letters can be incredibly powerful in shaping how your family remembers you—and how they carry on your legacy.

5. Philanthropy and Charitable Giving

If giving back is important to you, include:

- Donor-advised funds
- Charitable trusts
- Scholarships, endowments, or foundations

Teach your family how to evaluate charities and be intentional with giving.

6. Succession Planning for Business or Legal Practice

If you own a practice or legal consultancy:

- Create a transition plan
- Name and train a successor
- Document processes for a seamless exit

Having "The Talk" – Money Conversations with Your Family

Don't wait until a crisis to talk about money.
Schedule regular, age-appropriate conversations with your family:

- Explain what's in place and why
- Share your vision for their future
- Allow questions and input

Keep the tone open and non-judgmental. The goal is clarity and connection—not control.

How to Transfer Values Without Controlling Outcomes

- Share your story, not just your rules
- Give heirs decision-making experience while you're still around
- Make giving and saving a family tradition
- Use your will or trust to encourage education, service, or entrepreneurship

Tools to Consider

- Revocable Living Trusts
- Incentive Trusts (with guidelines for use)
- Family Foundations

- Legacy Letters
- Video messages or recorded interviews

Final Thoughts

Your legacy is more than your net worth. It's your worldview, your ethics, your story, and the example you've set.

Legacy planning lets you shape how you're remembered and how your resources are used long after you're gone. Done right, it can bind families closer, reduce confusion, and leave a lasting impact on causes and communities you care about.

Don't just leave valuables. Leave *values*. That's the true mark of a life well-lived—and a legacy well-planned.

Chapter 34: What Is the Market, the Economy, and Everything Else You See on TV?

Understanding the Financial Game: An Attorney's Guide to the Market

You've probably heard the headlines:

- "The market is crashing!"
- "The S&P 500 is on fire!"
- "The Fed hiked rates again!"
- "Inflation is spiraling!"

It's enough to make anyone want to ignore the noise and focus on billable hours, closing arguments, or prepping for your next deposition. But as an attorney, you know the importance of precedent, due diligence, and playing the long game.

Finance isn't that different.

Once you understand what's happening beneath the headlines, you'll see that the financial world — like the legal system — runs on structure, behavior, and long-term reasoning. And just like building a strong case, success in investing comes from discipline, not emotional reactions.

Let's break it down with comparisons that align with the way you think, work, and manage risk as a legal professional.

What Exactly Is the Stock Market?

The stock market is where people buy and sell shares of companies. Owning a share means you own a slice of that business. When the business grows, so does the value of your share.

Attorney Analogy: It's like holding equity in a firm. You're not just billing hours—you own part of the business. When the firm wins, so do you.

Why Do Markets Rise and Fall?

Prices move based on supply and demand. When more investors want to buy, prices go up. When more want to sell, they fall. Emotions, headlines, interest rates, and global politics can all influence this.

Attorney Analogy: Think of the market like a courtroom. There's strategy, conflict, unpredictability, and momentum. But you don't win cases by reacting emotionally—you stay grounded in the evidence.

Stock Market vs. Economy — What's the Difference?

The market reflects how investors *feel* about the future. The economy reflects what's *actually* happening: jobs, growth, productivity.

Attorney Analogy: It's like media spin versus courtroom facts. One is perception; one is proof. Smart investors—like great lawyers—analyze both.

Is Investing Risky? Can I Lose Everything?

Yes—if you go all in on a single stock or chase trends. But diversified investing (through index funds or ETFs) spreads risk and builds long-term strength.

Attorney Analogy: You don't base an entire case on one witness. You gather evidence, corroborate, and cross-check. Diversification is your case strategy.

Best Investment Strategy for Busy Attorneys?

Keep it simple:

- Low-cost index funds or ETFs
- Automatic monthly contributions
- Focus on the long-term

Attorney Analogy: Think of it like drafting a solid contract—no need for flash, just clarity, precision, and a plan that works over time.

When Should You Start?

As soon as possible.

The earlier you invest, the more compound growth works in your favor.

Attorney Analogy: You don't wait until trial day to prepare your brief. Early action wins cases—and builds wealth.

What Is the S&P 500?

It's an index of 500 of the largest U.S. companies. When people say "the market is up," this is usually what they mean.

Attorney Analogy: It's like the U.S. Supreme Court—highly influential, often used as a benchmark for the rest of the field.

Bull vs. Bear Markets

- Bull Market: Prices rising, optimism
- Bear Market: Prices falling, fear-driven

Attorney Analogy: A bull market is like winning streaks in court. A bear market is a tough season—you regroup, refine, and stick to your legal strategy.

Should You Sell When the Market Drops?

No—unless your strategy calls for it. Selling in panic just locks in losses.

Attorney Analogy: You wouldn't abandon a trial because of one bad ruling. You stick to your case and look at the total picture.

How Much Do You Need to Start?

As little as $50 or $100.

Many platforms allow fractional investing. You don't need a big win to begin building.

Attorney Analogy: Every strong case starts with a single fact. You build from there.

Day Trading vs. Long-Term Investing

Day trading is short-term speculation. Long-term investing is strategy.

Attorney Analogy: Day trading is chasing drama in court. Long-term investing is crafting a clear argument with solid precedent.

What's an ETF?

An Exchange-Traded Fund holds a collection of assets—like a bundle of stocks—traded as a single unit.

Attorney Analogy: Think of it as precedent law—you're relying on a body of cases rather than one unpredictable ruling.

Stocks vs. Bonds

- Stocks = ownership and growth potential
- Bonds = loan to a company or government, with fixed income

Attorney Analogy: Stocks are like litigation—higher reward, higher risk. Bonds are like structured settlements—steady, reliable, lower risk.

Diversification

Spreading your investments across different assets and sectors reduces risk.

Attorney Analogy: You don't argue from one statute or one case. You build a broad, defensible legal argument.

Should You Invest During a Downturn?

Yes. That's when investments are often "on sale."

Attorney Analogy: You don't stop building a case when a judge rules against you. You adapt and keep going.

Do Attorneys Need Financial Advisors?

You can start solo with platforms like Vanguard or Schwab. But as your practice grows or taxes get complex, a financial advisor becomes essential.

Attorney Analogy: You wouldn't represent yourself in a legal matter with real consequences. Same with high-stakes financial planning.

Final Thoughts: Build Your Financial Framework

The market isn't magic. It's not unfair. It's just unfamiliar—until you study it.

- Diversify like you prepare case law
- Stay consistent like billing hours
- Ignore noise, follow your strategy

- Check in annually, just like reviewing client files

The best investors, like the best lawyers, prepare, stay patient, and think long-term.

You've mastered legal briefs, oral arguments, and client advocacy. Now master the market.

Because the goal isn't just to earn a high income—it's to build a financially free future, one smart decision at a time.

Chapter 35: Student Loans – Strategies, Pitfalls, and Payoff Plans

Introduction: The Law Degree Price Tag

Becoming an attorney is a prestigious and intellectually demanding achievement—but it doesn't come cheap. The average law school graduate leaves with over $160,000 in student loan debt, often in addition to undergraduate loans. Factor in interest accumulation during law school and early career years, and many young attorneys find themselves burdened with loans exceeding $200,000 before they've even passed the bar.

This financial weight can delay life milestones—like buying a home, starting a family, or building wealth. It can also create emotional stress, imposter syndrome, and frustration at being "successful on paper" but broke in practice. This chapter breaks down your student loan options, repayment strategies, and how to make smart, empowering decisions from 3L year through partnership.

Section 1: Understanding Your Student Loans

Before you decide how to tackle them, you need to understand the types of loans you have.

Federal vs. Private Loans

- **Federal Loans**: Stafford (subsidized and unsubsidized), Grad PLUS, and Consolidation loans. These are eligible for income-driven repayment plans, PSLF, and deferment options.
- **Private Loans**: Issued by banks or other lenders. They usually have

fewer protections, no forgiveness, and limited repayment flexibility.

Loan Types

- **Direct Unsubsidized Loans**: Interest accrues from the time they're disbursed.
- **Grad PLUS Loans**: Higher interest rates and loan fees.
- **Perkins Loans**: Older, low-interest loans. If you have one, hang onto it—they're generally favorable.

Section 2: Early Career Moves – The First Five Years

The years after law school are pivotal for your financial trajectory.

Do: Enroll in an Income-Driven Repayment (IDR) Plan

- **SAVE (Successor to REPAYE)**: Lower payments, better interest subsidies.
- **PAYE or IBR**: Still options depending on when you borrowed.

Don't: Use Forbearance Without a Plan

- Forbearance pauses your payments—but interest continues to accrue.
- It's often offered quickly by loan servicers, but can lead to runaway balances.

Live Like a Law Student a Little Longer

- Avoid lifestyle inflation.
- Your income may rise quickly, but your debt won't vanish overnight.

Section 3: Forgiveness vs. Payoff – Which Path Is Yours?

Option 1: Public Service Loan Forgiveness (PSLF)

- 10 years of qualifying payments at a nonprofit or government employer.

- Tax-free forgiveness.

Great for attorneys at:

- Legal aid organizations
- Government agencies (city, state, federal)
- 501(c)(3) nonprofits

Do: Submit Employment Certification Forms (ECFs) annually. Don't: Assume your employer qualifies—verify it.

Option 2: Aggressive Repayment

- Ideal if you're going into BigLaw, corporate counsel, or a high-paying boutique.
- Allows you to refinance at a lower rate and eliminate debt quickly.

Do: Refinance after you're financially stable. Don't: Refinance federal loans if PSLF is still a possibility.

Section 4: Refinancing vs. Consolidation

Consolidation:

- Combines multiple federal loans into one.
- Retains federal protections and forgiveness eligibility.

Refinancing:

- Converts federal or private loans into a new private loan.
- Can lower interest rates.

Pros:

- Lower interest rate.
- May shorten repayment term.

Cons:

- No PSLF.
- Loss of federal protections.

Section 5: Loan Payoff Strategies

1. **Avalanche Method**: Focus on loans with highest interest rates.
2. **Snowball Method**: Focus on smallest balances for quick wins.
3. **Hybrid**: Prioritize based on a mix of rate, emotional burden, and flexibility.
4. **Biweekly Payments**: Makes an extra full payment per year.
5. **Lump Sums**: Use tax refunds, bonuses, or side hustle income.

Section 6: Do's and Don'ts

Do:

- Track loans at studentaid.gov
- Understand interest rates and capitalization
- Build an emergency fund
- Max out retirement while paying loans, if possible
- Read fine print on refinancing

Don't:

- Ignore loans for years
- Miss payments or recertification deadlines
- Assume PSLF is automatic
- Let others' strategies dictate your own

Section 7: Case Studies

1. **The PSLF Attorney** Lisa worked at a public defender's office for 10

years, submitted ECFs annually, and had $160K forgiven. She stayed in IDR the entire time and lived below her means.

2. **The BigLaw Payer** Mark entered BigLaw with $180K debt. He refinanced to a 3.5% loan once he made partner and paid it off in five years while maxing out his 401(k).
3. **The Missed Opportunity** Tina took a fellowship at a nonprofit but didn't certify for PSLF. Later refinanced her loans after moving to the private sector. She missed out on nearly $70K in forgiveness.

Section 8: Advanced Planning Moves

- **Married Filing Separately**: Could lower IDR payments (but check the tax tradeoffs).
- **PSLF for Two**: Married attorneys at nonprofits? Coordinate your strategy.
- **Employer Repayment Perks**: Some firms and agencies offer $5K–$20K+ annually.
- **Firm Bonuses**: Negotiate sign-on or year-end bonuses to help wipe out debt faster.

Section 9: Common Pitfalls

- Refinancing too early
- Forgetting to recertify income for IDR
- Not reading your servicer emails
- Not building wealth alongside loan payoff
- Letting anxiety paralyze decision-making

Section 10: Mindset

You didn't go to law school to live paycheck to paycheck for the next 20 years. Student loans are a hurdle—not a life sentence. With a clear plan, they become just another part of your financial journey.

Build a plan. Automate it. Live your life.

And remember: the best investment you've already made is in yourself. Now make sure it pays off.

Chapter 36: Taking Investment Advice from Other Attorneys: The Pros, Cons, and Rules of Thumb

Title: Taking Investment Advice from Fellow Attorneys: Smart or Risky?

Introduction: When Smart People Give Questionable Financial Advice As an attorney, you're surrounded by highly educated peers who excel at critical thinking, problem-solving, and navigating high-stakes environments. It's natural to seek advice from fellow lawyers when managing your finances—especially investments. After all, they understand the unique demands, billing structures, and financial pressures that come with the legal profession.

However, while your colleagues may offer valuable insights based on their personal experiences, relying solely on investment advice from fellow attorneys—particularly those who don't use financial advisors—can lead to unintended financial consequences. In this chapter, we'll examine the appeal, benefits, and potential pitfalls of taking financial cues from peers, and outline smart ways to protect your financial future.

Why Attorneys Turn to Each Other for Advice

1. Shared Professional Experience Attorneys understand the industry's financial rhythms: student loan debt, late starts to earning, variable income based on bonuses, contingency fees, or self-employment. Peer advice often feels more relatable than advice from a generalist financial

advisor.

2. Trust and Accessibility The legal field thrives on trust and reputation. If a successful colleague is investing in real estate or crypto, it s tempting to follow their lead. There's no fee attached, and you might feel more comfortable discussing money with a peer than with a paid advisor.
3. Real-Life Examples Peers may share success stories or strategies that worked well for them. Hearing firsthand how someone paid off debt quickly or bought into a partnership can inspire action.

Pros of Peer-Based Financial Advice

- **Cost-Free Insight**: Advice from a peer comes without advisor fees or commissions.
- **Tailored Context**: Another lawyer may understand your cash flow, tax bracket, or partnership track better than someone outside the profession.
- **Emotional Support**: Having a financial sounding board you trust can reduce decision paralysis.

The Risks of Following Fellow Attorneys

1. **Lack of Expertise** Legal expertise does not equal financial expertise. Even if a colleague appears successful, they may lack deep understanding of diversification, tax optimization, or long-term planning. They may also underestimate risk due to overconfidence in their own judgment.
2. **Bias Toward Familiar Investments** Attorneys often invest in what they know: law firm buy-ins, real estate, or passive business interests. These may not be diversified or suitable for your situation.
3. **No Holistic View** A peer may offer a good idea in isolation—like buying a rental property—but ignore how that investment fits within your retirement plan, estate strategy, or insurance needs.
4. **Conflicts of Interest** A colleague might recommend investing in their

own business venture or project. Their advice may not be impartial, even if well-intended.

5. **Herd Mentality and Pressure to Imitate** It's easy to feel behind if others are investing in startups, syndications, or private equity. But their choices may be driven more by ego or fear of missing out than financial logic.

Rules of Thumb Before Taking Peer Advice

- **Ask Questions**: What is their experience? What's the downside? How does this fit into a long-term plan?
- **Don't Imitate—Evaluate**: Their income, liabilities, goals, and risk tolerance aren't yours.
- **Check the Source**: Are they relying on a professional or going it alone?
- **Verify with an Expert**: A CFP, CPA, or fiduciary advisor can help you stress-test peer ideas.
- **Avoid Groupthink**: Just because five attorneys at your firm are in a certain deal doesn't mean it's right for you.

Better Alternatives

- Work with a fee-only financial advisor who understands high-income professionals.
- Invest in low-cost index funds or ETFs tailored to your time horizon.
- Maximize tax-advantaged accounts like 401(k)s, Roth IRAs (or backdoor Roths), HSAs, and defined benefit plans.
- Diversify: balance real estate, equities, bonds, and cash reserves.

Conclusion: Advice Should Be Grounded, Not Just Trusted Colleagues can offer encouragement, ideas, and perspective—but they shouldn't be your only financial guide. When it comes to your wealth, take the same approach you use in law: gather evidence, consider precedent, understand your risk, and seek expert counsel.

Listen to your peers, but verify with professionals. Invest not just with your income—but with intention.

Chapter 37: Should Attorneys Invest in Land?

Land investment is often praised as a reliable long-term strategy for building wealth. It's tangible. It's limited. And in many cases, it appreciates steadily over time. For attorneys—especially those with rising incomes and long-term goals—land can offer a unique and potentially lucrative way to diversify a portfolio. But it also comes with risks that don't always get the attention they deserve.

This chapter will break down the pros and cons of investing in land, how it compares to other investments, and whether it's a smart move for attorneys looking to build generational wealth without overextending themselves.

What Is Land Investment?

Land investment refers to the purchase of undeveloped or minimally developed property with the expectation of future appreciation or income. Unlike traditional real estate, such as rental homes or commercial buildings, land often produces little or no cash flow and may require a longer time horizon to realize gains.

Types of land include:

- **Raw land**: Completely undeveloped land, no utilities or infrastructure.
- **Agricultural land**: Used for farming, ranching, or leasing to agricultural operators.

- **Development land**: Parcels expected to be re-zoned or built upon in the future.
- **Recreational land**: Used for hunting, fishing, or private retreats.
- **Timberland**: Forested land harvested for lumber over time.

Benefits of Land Investment

1. Tangible, Scarce Asset

Land is physical. You can walk on it, fence it, and own something that isn't going anywhere. There's a psychological comfort in owning a piece of the earth, and that's part of the appeal. Because land is limited—especially in growing markets—demand often increases as population and development expand.

2. Long-Term Appreciation Potential

While land may not explode in value overnight, it can increase steadily, especially in areas near infrastructure, highways, or residential growth. This slow-but-steady growth makes land attractive for attorneys with long-term investment goals and a stable income base.

3. Low Maintenance Requirements

Unlike rental property, you don't have tenants, repairs, or management headaches. There's no plumbing to fix, no roofs to patch, and no leases to negotiate. Outside of property taxes and minimal upkeep (think mowing or clearing brush), it's a largely hands-off investment.

4. Portfolio Diversification

Most attorneys invest in stocks, bonds, or law firm equity. Land moves independently from financial markets, offering a hedge during market volatility or economic downturns. It adds a layer of security and diversification to an investment mix that may be overly dependent on Wall Street.

5. Flexible Exit Strategies

Land gives you options: hold and wait, lease it for farming, timber, or recreation, develop it yourself, or sell to a builder or investor. You don't have to choose just one. Attorneys with strategic vision can use land in creative ways to support estate planning or long-term passive income.

Drawbacks of Land Investment

1. Illiquidity

Land is hard to sell quickly. It's not like stocks or even rental properties with consistent buyer demand. If you need fast cash, unloading a land parcel could take months or years—especially if it's remote or zoned for limited use.

2. No Immediate Income

Most land doesn't produce monthly income unless it's leased out for farming or recreational use. This lack of cash flow can feel frustrating—especially for attorneys used to a regular paycheck or those looking for income-generating investments.

3. Ongoing Costs

Even unused land carries costs: property taxes, liability insurance, legal compliance, or land management. These can add up over time, especially in high-tax jurisdictions or areas with changing zoning laws.

4. Zoning and Legal Restrictions

Land use is tightly regulated by local governments. Buying a parcel doesn't guarantee you can build on it, develop it, or even access utilities. Attorneys must do serious due diligence—including legal review—to avoid buying land that's unusable for its intended purpose.

5. Speculative Nature

Land is a bet on the future. Will development head your way? Will zoning change? Will a new highway or commercial corridor improve its value? There's no guarantee. And speculation—while sometimes rewarding—comes with risk.

How to Evaluate Land as an Attorney

Start by asking yourself:

- Can I afford to let this money sit for 10+ years?
- Am I looking for cash flow, or am I okay with delayed returns?
- Do I have time to do proper due diligence?
- Am I investing near where I live—or relying on third-hand info?
- Could this money be better used in my practice, retirement accounts, or other assets?

Land makes sense **if** you've covered your financial bases: maxed out retirement accounts, built a cash reserve, and paid down high-interest debt. Only then should you consider tying up capital in something long-term and illiquid.

Better Land Buys for Attorneys

If you're still interested, here are some lower-risk ways to invest in land:

- **Buy land near urban expansion**: Target areas where infrastructure is being built, zoning changes are in the works, or residential growth is expected.
- **Lease it for farming or hunting**: This offsets taxes and maintenance while you wait for appreciation.
- **Buy with a partner**: Split the cost and spread the risk—just have a legal agreement in place.
- **Use a land-focused REIT**: If you want exposure to land without buying it outright, real estate investment trusts that focus on farmland or timberland can provide passive exposure with liquidity.

Final Thoughts

Land can be an excellent wealth-building tool—but it's not for everyone. For attorneys with long-term vision, excess capital, and the willingness to research zoning and local development, it can add significant value to an already strong portfolio. But it's not a substitute for retirement savings, paying down debt, or investing in yourself or your practice.

If you do pursue land, treat it like you would any other case—gather facts, assess risks, look for blind spots, and consult professionals. That kind of disciplined thinking is what makes good attorneys—and smart investors.

Chapter 38: Common Mistakes Attorneys Make with Money

And How to Avoid Them

Even the most brilliant legal minds can make basic financial errors. The problem isn't intelligence—it's inattention, time pressure, and a professional culture that rewards short-term wins over long-term planning.

Here are some of the most common financial missteps attorneys make—and how to sidestep them.

1. Waiting Too Long to Start Saving or Investing

The Mistake: Many attorneys delay financial planning because of student debt or the belief that "real money" comes later.

The Fix: Start where you are. Even small amounts invested early benefit from decades of compound interest. Don't wait for the perfect time—it rarely comes.

2. Lifestyle Creep

The Mistake: As income increases, spending rises to match. New cars, upgraded homes, and luxury vacations become "needs" instead of choices.

The Fix: Set savings goals before you increase your spending. Automate investments and delay major lifestyle upgrades until your foundation is solid.

3. Ignoring Student Loans

The Mistake: Making minimum payments without a strategy, or refinancing federal loans without understanding the risks.

The Fix: Understand your repayment options, forgiveness programs, and whether refinancing is right for your career path. A customized strategy can save you thousands.

4. Overestimating Job Security

The Mistake: Assuming a law firm job will always be there—and not preparing for downturns, layoffs, or health issues.

The Fix: Build an emergency fund (3–6 months minimum) and invest in disability insurance, especially if you're the primary breadwinner.

5. Failing to Set a Financial Plan

The Mistake: Working hard without clear financial goals, resulting in high income but low net worth.

The Fix: Create a roadmap with targets for savings, debt repayment, investing, and retirement. You need more than income—you need a plan.

6. Not Understanding Their Compensation

The Mistake: Many attorneys don't fully understand their salary structure, bonus terms, partnership track, or benefits like equity or profit-sharing.

The Fix: Learn the full details of your compensation package and use that info to negotiate and plan your finances more effectively.

7. Skipping Basic Insurance

The Mistake: Avoiding disability, life, or umbrella insurance because "it won't happen to me."

The Fix: As your income grows, so should your protection. Insurance is a financial backstop—not an expense to avoid.

8. Doing It All Themselves

The Mistake: Attorneys often think, "I'm smart, I'll figure it out," and avoid hiring advisors.

The Fix: Partner with professionals—financial planners, CPAs, and estate attorneys—who can help you make better, faster decisions.

9. Chasing Hot Investments or Trends

The Mistake: Jumping into crypto, stock tips, or real estate flips without due diligence.

The Fix: Stick to a diversified strategy rooted in fundamentals. Investing isn't supposed to be exciting—it's supposed to work.

10. Neglecting Estate and Legacy Planning

The Mistake: Thinking wills and trusts are for "later" or for other people.

The Fix: Create a basic estate plan now—especially if you have a family, assets, or student loans with a cosigner. Your legacy starts today.

Bottom Line

You've built a career on logic, discipline, and planning. Apply those same strengths to your finances—and you'll not only earn well but *keep and grow* what you earn.

Avoiding these common traps can be the difference between a high-income lifestyle and true financial freedom.

Chapter 39: Do Attorneys Need a Financial Advisor? Weighing the Pros, Cons, and Key Considerations

As an attorney, you are trained to manage complexity, assess risk, and interpret fine print. You're accustomed to solving other people's problems—negotiating settlements, navigating contracts, and defending rights. With that in mind, it's tempting to believe that you can manage your finances solo. After all, you've made it through law school, passed the bar, and survived endless billable hours—how hard can financial planning really be?

But here's the truth: just because you're intelligent and analytical doesn't mean you're equipped to manage all aspects of your financial life alone. Attorneys are often excellent at generating income, but that doesn't automatically translate to building wealth, minimizing taxes, or preparing for long-term goals like retirement, college savings, or practice succession.

This chapter explores whether hiring a financial advisor makes sense for you, outlines the benefits and drawbacks, and offers clear guidance for attorneys at every stage of their career.

The Case for DIY Financial Planning

Let's acknowledge the obvious first: some attorneys absolutely can—and do—manage their own finances effectively. Here's why DIY might work for you:

- **You're deeply interested in personal finance.** You read financial blogs, follow investment news, and have a firm handle on budgeting, saving, and retirement planning.
- **You have a straightforward financial situation.** No kids, no business interests, no multiple income streams—just a W-2 job and a 401(k).
- **You enjoy control and independence.** You'd rather do the research yourself than pay someone else to manage your money.
- **You want to save on fees.** Advisors can charge 1% or more of your assets under management (AUM) or bill hourly or by flat fee. If you're confident in your skills, avoiding those costs can seem appealing.

But here's the challenge: as your career, wealth, and family grow, your financial situation becomes more complex—fast.

When Hiring a Financial Advisor Starts Making Sense

For most attorneys, the tipping point comes when you start juggling more than just a paycheck. You may:

- Launch your own practice or buy into a firm.
- Inherit assets or manage trust distributions.
- Save for your kids' college while still paying off your own student loans.
- Earn equity compensation or non-traditional income from consulting, teaching, or board roles.
- Need help navigating tax strategy, charitable giving, or estate planning.

A good financial advisor doesn't just "manage your investments." They help coordinate every aspect of your financial life—investments, insurance, taxes, business planning, retirement, and wealth transfer.

Pros of Hiring a Financial Advisor

1. Strategic Planning Across Multiple Goals

A financial advisor can help you create a roadmap that ties together short-term goals (like buying a home), medium-term goals (like saving for your child's college), and long-term goals (like retiring early or passing on wealth efficiently).

They help prioritize where to allocate your dollars—should you pay off debt, invest more, max out retirement accounts, or contribute to a 529 plan?

2. Tax Optimization

Attorneys often miss major tax-saving opportunities. A financial advisor—especially one who works closely with CPAs—can help you:

- Strategically time income and deductions
- Use tax-loss harvesting or Roth conversions
- Maximize charitable contributions
- Structure tax-efficient withdrawals in retirement

3. Portfolio Management

Many attorneys invest reactively rather than with a strategy. An advisor ensures your investments align with your goals, risk tolerance, and time horizon.

They also handle rebalancing, keep emotions in check during market volatility, and help you avoid common behavioral mistakes (like panic selling).

4. Coordination With Other Professionals

The best advisors don't work in silos. They collaborate with your estate planning attorney, CPA, insurance agent, and—if you own a practice—your business consultant.

This integrated approach ensures your entire financial picture is optimized, not just your portfolio.

5. Accountability and Peace of Mind

Much like your clients rely on you to help them navigate legal risk, you can rely on a financial advisor to keep your goals on track, avoid blind spots, and challenge decisions when emotions creep in.

Sometimes, having someone objective in your corner is the difference between staying the course and making a costly mistake.

Cons of Hiring a Financial Advisor

1. Cost

Advisors typically charge:

- **1.25% of assets under management (AUM)**
- **Flat annual fees** ($2,000–$10,000 depending on complexity)
- **Hourly rates** ($150–$500/hour)

If you don't need much ongoing support or have limited assets, that cost might outweigh the benefit—especially early in your career.

2. Quality Varies

Not all advisors are created equal. Some are salespeople in disguise, pushing annuities or high-commission products.

That's why it's critical to:

- Choose a **fiduciary** (legally obligated to act in your best interest)
- Look for credentials like **CFP®**, **CPA**, or **CFA**
- Understand how they get paid (fee-only is best for objectivity)

3. Over-Reliance

Some clients delegate so much that they stop engaging altogether. That's risky. Even with an advisor, you should understand the basics—after all, you're still the CEO of your own financial life.

How to Know If You're Ready for an Advisor

Ask yourself:

- Are my finances getting too complex to manage alone?
- Do I have significant income, assets, or a major life transition coming up?
- Am I confident that my investment, tax, and estate strategies are aligned?
- Do I have time to research financial issues—or am I procrastinating important decisions?
- Would I benefit from an expert perspective, especially during uncertain markets?

If you answered yes to most of these, it may be time to explore hiring an advisor.

What Kind of Advisor Should You Hire?

Fee-Only Financial Planner

- Fiduciary
- Charges flat fee, hourly, or percentage of assets
- No commissions or product sales
- Best for objective advice

Wealth Manager

- Offers planning + investment management
- Good for attorneys with >$500K–$1M in investable assets
- Often includes tax, estate, and legacy planning

Specialist in Attorney/Professional Clients

Some advisors work exclusively with attorneys, physicians, or other high-income professionals. They understand unique cash flow, partnership, and tax structures.

Ask:

- "Do you work with other attorneys?"
- "How do you tailor strategies to legal professionals?"

Alternatives to Full-Time Advisors

If you're not ready to commit to a long-term relationship, consider:

- **One-time financial plan**: A flat-fee consultation to review goals, strategy, and next steps.
- **Hourly check-ins**: Meet once or twice a year for strategy and accountability.
- **Robo-advisors**: Low-cost platforms like Betterment or Wealthfront that offer automated investing with optional human guidance.

Conclusion: Advisors Don't Replace You—They Empower You

Hiring a financial advisor doesn't mean giving up control. It means **taking responsibility** for your future by building the right team—just like your clients do when they hire you.

An advisor's job isn't to make decisions for you, but to **equip you** with insights, accountability, and structure so that you make better ones.

If you're serious about turning your income into long-term wealth—and designing a life that serves your values, goals, and legacy—it may be time to get help. Not because you can't do it yourself…

But because you have more important things to do with your time.

And in the end, the smartest people know when to call in another professional.

Chapter 40: Family Law Awareness (Even if You're Not a Divorce Attorney)

Protecting Your Wealth, Relationships, and Future Through Life's Most Common Legal Event

You may never practice family law, but **you can't afford to ignore it**—because whether you're a litigator, transactional attorney, partner, or solo practitioner, the legal and financial consequences of marriage, divorce, or blended families can profoundly affect your wealth, cash flow, estate plan, and legacy.

This chapter isn't just for those going through divorce. It's for every lawyer who is—or will be—married, remarried, co-parenting, or supporting a family. Understanding the **financial implications of family law** can help you protect your assets, prepare responsibly, and avoid devastating missteps when life doesn't go as planned.

1. How Divorce Impacts Wealth, Cash Flow, and Retirement

Divorce is more than a legal process—it's a financial earthquake. And for attorneys, especially those with high incomes or equity interests in a firm, the fallout can be significant.

Key Financial Risks in Divorce:

- **Division of marital assets**, including retirement accounts, investments, and real estate
- **Loss of liquidity** due to legal fees, buyouts, and temporary support
- **Spousal support (alimony)** and **child support** obligations that can extend for years
- **Impact on retirement timelines** due to asset depletion
- **Reduced credit access** and new housing/insurance costs

Common Financial Mistakes:

- Underestimating the true cost of divorce (average legal fees: $15,000–$50,000+)
- Failing to understand how income is treated for support purposes (e.g., bonuses, stock options)
- Not accounting for **qualified domestic relations orders (QDROs)** when dividing retirement accounts
- Ignoring the **long-term compounding loss** of split investment portfolios

Planning Tips:

- If divorce is a possibility, consult a **divorce financial planner** or family law attorney early
- Document your **assets and debts thoroughly**
- Know the value of your **firm equity, pension, or buyout rights**
- Consider whether a **postnuptial agreement** might protect future income

2. Prenuptial and Postnuptial Agreements: More Than Just "Rich People Documents"

As an attorney, you understand contracts. A **prenuptial agreement** is simply a contract between two people entering marriage that defines how assets, debts, and income will be treated in case of divorce or death.

Why Lawyers Should Consider Prenups or Postnups:

- You have (or expect to have) **significant earnings or assets**
- You have children from a previous relationship
- You own part of a **law firm, practice, or business**
- Your spouse has debt or financial obligations you don't want to absorb
- You want clarity and control—not confusion—in the event of separation

Prenup vs. Postnup:

- **Prenup** = Signed before marriage
- **Postnup** = Signed after marriage, often used during reconciliation, transition, or after major financial events

Note: These documents must be negotiated fairly, with full disclosure, and ideally with both parties represented by counsel to hold up in court.

3. Estate and Trust Planning During or After Divorce

Divorce is a trigger event that **requires a full review of your estate plan**. Failing to update your documents and beneficiaries can have lasting consequences.

Key Areas to Revisit:

- **Wills and trusts**: Remove ex-spouse, reassign guardianship for children
- **Beneficiary designations**: Update retirement accounts, life insurance, brokerage accounts
- **Durable powers of attorney** and **healthcare proxies**: These often name a spouse—reassign immediately after separation
- **Trust structures**: If your children are minors or if remarriage is in your future, consider a revocable or irrevocable trust to protect assets

Advanced Strategies:

- Consider a **spousal lifetime access trust (SLAT)** if remarried
- Use **irrevocable life insurance trusts (ILITs)** to protect assets from estate tax while ensuring children or dependents are provided for
- Create **special needs or educational trusts** for children with additional planning needs

4. Custody and Financial Obligations: Child Support, Alimony, and Education Planning

Child Support:

- Based on **income, custody time, and number of children**
- Often **non-negotiable** and determined by statutory guidelines
- Includes provisions for healthcare, childcare, and sometimes extracurriculars

Spousal Support (Alimony):

- Varies by state: may be temporary, rehabilitative, or long-term
- Based on **earning capacity**, length of marriage, and standard of living
- May phase out upon remarriage or after a fixed term

Education Planning:

- In many states, parents may be **required to contribute to college costs**
- **529 plans** should be addressed in divorce agreements—who owns them, who contributes, and how funds are used
- Consider joint agreements on **school choice, tuition, and private education**

Note: Financial obligations don't end at age 18. Smart planning can prevent conflict years after the divorce is finalized.

5. Even If You're Not Getting Divorced: Plan Like You Might Be

Most lawyers wouldn't show up in court without a written argument—but many go into marriage without any plan for financial separation, asset protection, or exit strategy.

Questions Every Attorney Should Ask (Regardless of Marital Status):

- If I died tomorrow, would my spouse know how to access our financial accounts?
- If I got divorced next year, would I be able to untangle my finances smoothly?
- If I remarried, how would I protect my children's inheritance?
- Do I understand the marital laws in my state (community property vs. equitable distribution)?
- Have I separated my premarital assets and documented ownership?

You don't need to expect the worst—you just need to **prepare responsibly**. Your clients plan for risk. You should, too.

Final Thoughts: Marriage Is Emotional. Divorce Is Financial.

Whether you're newly married, ten years into a partnership, or on your second chapter, understanding how **family law intersects with financial planning** is essential—not just for your peace of mind, but for protecting your legacy.

You may never litigate a divorce case, but you will **live through the consequences** of the financial choices you make in your personal life. The attorneys who thrive in their careers—and in life—are those who understand how to structure their wealth, protect their families, and prepare for the unexpected.

Because at the end of the day, it's not just about protecting your assets. It's about protecting **your future, your freedom, and your family.**

Chapter 41: Conclusion You've Mastered the Law—Now Master Your Wealth

Conclusion Chapter: Financial Literacy for Attorneys

You've Mastered the Law. Now Master Your Wealth.

You didn't go to law school just to make money. You went because you wanted to advocate for others, solve problems, and make a meaningful impact. Yet, the legal profession—despite all its intellectual rewards—can often leave even the sharpest minds unprepared for their own financial future. Law school trains you to argue case law, interpret contracts, and analyze precedent. But who trained you to manage six figures of student debt? Who taught you how to read a 401(k) statement? Who explained the difference between term and permanent life insurance or the real cost of delayed investing?

If you're like most attorneys, you figured it out on your own—or not at all. That's why this book exists. Not to shame you for what you don't know, but to empower you with what you should.

This conclusion is not the end of your journey; it's the start of your next chapter. And whether you're a first-year associate still getting your financial feet under you, a mid-career partner juggling competing priorities, or a seasoned litigator thinking about retirement, this moment is an opportunity to reflect, recalibrate, and re-engage with your financial life in a way that builds both security and significance.

What You've Learned

Throughout this book, we've explored every major financial domain that matters to attorneys. You've learned how to:

- Assess the true cost of your legal education and navigate repayment strategies
- Build a real-world budget that accounts for irregular income, billable hours, and lifestyle inflation
- Understand and negotiate compensation—whether you're at BigLaw, a boutique firm, solo practice, government, or in-house
- Master tax basics and avoid common filing mistakes lawyers make
- Choose insurance policies that actually fit your life—not just the ones pushed on you
- Invest with intention, diversify wisely, and avoid high-fee traps
- Prepare for retirement while balancing competing priorities like buying a home, starting a family, or opening a practice
- Protect your wealth through estate planning, asset protection, and long-term care planning
- Identify red flags in investments, and avoid bad advice from well-meaning (but ill-informed) colleagues
- Set boundaries with friends and family, especially when you're the first to "make it"
- Build multiple income streams, including passive options that complement your law career
- Recognize the impact of burnout, stress, and mental health on financial decision-making

The point wasn't to make you a financial advisor. The point was to give you the knowledge and clarity you need to become your own best advocate—for your future, your goals, your peace of mind.

The Unique Financial Landscape of Legal Professionals

Being a lawyer comes with financial challenges that many other professionals simply don't face:

- **Delayed earnings:** You started earning real income later than your peers in other fields. Many of your friends from undergrad were already on their third promotion while you were still preparing for the bar.
- **Student loan burdens:** Six-figure debt is the norm. With law school tuition, bar exam prep, and cost of living, many attorneys start their careers in a deep financial hole.
- **Variable income:** Bonuses, contingent fees, inconsistent client retainers—your income might spike one month and dip the next.
- **High cost of success:** The lifestyle creep is real. Designer suits, business lunches, a nicer car for client impressions. In law, optics matter—but that doesn't mean you should go broke trying to look the part.
- **Burnout risk:** Long hours, client demands, and billable pressures can lead to financial procrastination, poor spending habits, and neglect of long-term planning.
- **Complex family and estate dynamics:** Many attorneys have aging parents, children heading to college, or complicated family structures that require advanced planning.

Financial literacy isn't just about money. It's about understanding how to design a life that aligns with your values, your responsibilities, and your goals—and doing it on purpose.

Rewriting Your Money Story

Lawyers are storytellers. We take facts, organize them into a narrative, and advocate for a better outcome. But have you ever stopped to ask yourself: **What story are you telling yourself about money?**

- Were you raised in a home where money was a source of stress?
- Did your parents avoid talking about finances?
- Do you feel guilt around making more than your family members?
- Do you overspend to self-soothe from career burnout?
- Are you avoiding financial planning because it triggers anxiety?

These patterns don't make you weak. They make you human. But the longer you let those stories go unchallenged, the more power they have over your financial future.

It's time to rewrite the script.

You don't have to know everything. You just have to care enough to ask better questions. You have to recognize that financial planning is not something to avoid—it's something to embrace.

Because if you don't decide what your money is going to do, someone else will.

The Wealth Formula for Attorneys

You don't need a complex financial playbook to succeed. Most financially successful attorneys follow a few timeless principles:

1. **Spend less than you earn.**
2. **Invest the difference early and often.**
3. **Use insurance to protect what you can't afford to lose.**
4. **Avoid debt unless it creates leverage or opportunity.**
5. **Make financial decisions with your future self in mind.**

That's it.

You don't need to chase crypto. You don't need a private equity deal. You don't need to time the market or pick stocks. You just need a system.

And if you don't have time to manage that system on your own? Hire someone. Find a fiduciary advisor who understands attorneys. Build a financial team like you would build a legal team: with strategy, alignment, and trust.

From Confusion to Confidence

Think back to your first day of law school. How overwhelmed you felt. How many acronyms you didn't understand. How strange it felt to brief a case or cold-call in front of your peers.

Now look at you. Confident. Strategic. Respected. That's not because the material got easier—it's because **you got stronger.**

The same thing will happen with your finances.

You don't need to have it all figured out. You just need to start. Bit by bit. Week by week. One smart decision at a time.

- Open that investment account
- Increase your retirement contribution by 1%
- Set up a will and healthcare proxy
- Track your spending for 30 days
- Hire a professional for things you're ready to delegate

Each step is a vote for the kind of life you want. Each decision is a brick in the financial foundation of your future.

The Power of Financial Peace

What does wealth actually mean to you?

- Is it being able to retire early?
- Taking a sabbatical without fear?
- Paying for your kids' college in cash?
- Supporting a cause you care deeply about?
- Traveling for pleasure instead of out of obligation?

Wealth isn't just a number. It's freedom. It's time. It's control.

When you stop living paycheck to paycheck—even if those paychecks are big ones—you gain something far more valuable than a nicer car or a bigger home. You gain **peace of mind.**

And in a career as high-stakes as law, peace of mind is priceless.

A Final Word to Young Attorneys

If you're early in your career and overwhelmed, hear this:

You are not behind. You are not dumb for not knowing this yet. You are not broken because you feel stressed about money.

But now is the best time to begin. The habits you form in your 20s and 30s will define your financial trajectory far more than any one job or salary.

Start small. Build the habit. Stack wins.

You don't have to become a financial genius. But you do need to become a financial **participant.**

A Final Word to Seasoned Attorneys

If you're further along in your career, you may be asking:

"Is it too late for me to change?" "Should I have more saved by now?" "What if I've already made some mistakes?"

Here's the truth:

It's never too late to get intentional. It's never too late to plan for the next chapter. It's never too late to turn around and teach the next generation of lawyers what you wish you had known.

You still have time to protect what you've built, align your wealth with your values, and leave a legacy you're proud of.

Final Checklist: Financial Wins to Prioritize Next

- Build a real, values-based budget
- Create a 3-6 month emergency fund
- Max out your 401(k) or 403(b)

- Open and fund a Roth IRA (or backdoor Roth if needed)
- Set clear short- and long-term financial goals
- Get adequate life, disability, and liability insurance
- Meet with a fiduciary financial advisor
- Draft (or update) your will and healthcare directives
- Pay off high-interest debt
- Learn about charitable giving, estate planning, and trusts

Each item you check off moves you closer to freedom.

Your Legacy Starts Now

Money isn't the point.

What money makes possible is.

This is your invitation to lead with vision. To let your financial life reflect your legal life—organized, thoughtful, intentional.

You already know how to protect your clients. Now protect yourself.

You already know how to argue for justice. Now argue for your own well-being.

You already know how to fight for what matters. Now fight for the financial life you've earned.

This is not just about being rich.

It's about being ready.

It's about being free.

It's about finally living the life you worked so hard to build.

And it starts today.

Congratulations. You're not just an attorney. You're now a financially literate one.

Let's build something that lasts.

Questions for Financial Advisors and CPA's

10 Questions to Ask a Financial Advisor

1. **Are you a fiduciary 100% of the time—and can you put that in writing?**
2. *(This ensures they are legally obligated to act in your best interest.)*
3. **How are you compensated? Fee-only, commission, or fee-based?**
4. *(Transparency on fees helps you avoid hidden costs or product-driven advice.)*
5. **Do you specialize in working with attorneys or other high-income professionals?**
6. *(An advisor familiar with your career structure will better understand your financial needs.)*
7. **What licenses or certifications do you hold? (e.g., CFP®, CFA, ChFC)**
8. *(Credentials matter. Look for advisors with fiduciary-level certifications.)*
9. **What services are included in your planning? (e.g., retirement, tax strategy, estate coordination, insurance?)**
10. *(Ensure they provide holistic advice, not just investment management.)*
11. **What is your investment philosophy and approach to risk management?**
12. *(You want to understand if their strategy aligns with your goals and temperament.)*
13. **How will we communicate, and how often do we review or update my financial plan?**

14. (*Regular check-ins are essential as your life and income change*)
15. **How do you handle tax-efficient investing and portfolio rebalancing?**
16. (*A tax-aware investment strategy is crucial for attorneys in higher brackets.*)
17. **Can you help with employee benefits, deferred compensation, or law firm retirement plans?**
18. (*Many attorneys need help navigating unique compensation structures.*)
19. **What happens if I decide to stop working with you? Are there exit fees or restrictions on transferring my assets?**
20. (*You should have the freedom to leave without penalty.*)

10 Questions to Ask a CPA / Tax Advisor

1. **Do you specialize in working with attorneys, law firms, or professional service providers?**
2. (*Industry experience ensures a better understanding of write-offs, compensation, and firm ownership.*)
3. **What services do you provide beyond tax preparation? (e.g., tax planning, audit support, consulting)**
4. (*Tax planning is year-round. A great CPA does more than file forms.*)
5. **How do you charge for your services—flat fee, hourly, or retainer?**
6. (*Understand your costs and whether planning and filing are bundled.*)
7. **Can you help me minimize taxes on W-2, 1099, K-1, and investment income?**
8. (*Attorneys often have complex income types—your CPA should understand all of them.*)
9. **What's your approach to working with other professionals like financial advisors or estate attorneys?**
10. (*You want a collaborative partner who helps coordinate your financial team.*)
11. **Can you help me with multi-state tax issues, estimated payments, or self-employment income?**
12. (*This is especially important for attorneys who relocate, do contract work, or*

operate solo practices.)

13. **How do you stay current on new tax laws that affect high-income professionals or business owners?**
14. (*Tax law changes quickly—ongoing education is key.*)
15. **Do you have experience with charitable giving, donor-advised funds, or tax-advantaged trusts?**
16. (*Look for advisors who can support your long-term legacy and giving goals.*)
17. **Can you assist with tax strategies related to retirement accounts, RMDs, and Roth conversions?**
18. (*Attorneys in their 40s–60s often need long-term distribution strategies.*)
19. **What happens if I get audited or receive a notice from the IRS—do you provide audit representation or support?**
20. (*You need to know if your CPA will stand by you if the IRS comes knocking.*)

Annual Financial Calendar – Important Dates Every Attorney Should Know

JANUARY

- **January 1**
- New contribution limits for **401(k), 403(b), 457**, and **IRA/Roth IRA** go into effect.
- **Health Savings Account (HSA)** and **Flexible Spending Account (FSA)** limits reset.
- Begin **new year's budget and cash flow review**.
- Update **paycheck withholding (Form W-4)** if you've had life changes.
- **January 15**
- **4th Quarter Estimated Taxes Due** (for income earned October 1 – December 31 of previous year). Use IRS Form 1040-ES.
- **Late January**
- Begin receiving **W-2s, 1099-NEC, 1099-MISC, 1099-INT, 1099-DIV, and 1099-B** from employers, banks, brokerages, and clients.

FEBRUARY

- **February 1**
- Deadline for employers and payers to issue **W-2s and 1099s** to employees and contractors.
- **Mid to Late February**
- Receive **K-1s** from partnerships or S-corporations (may be delayed into

March or April).

- Start preparing documentation for **tax filing** or submission to your CPA.

MARCH

- **March 15**
- **Partnership and S-Corporation Tax Returns Due (Form 1065 or 1120-S).**
- (Can file extension using Form 7004.)
- **March 31**
- Last day to receive **electronic** Form 1095-A, 1095-B, or 1095-C (health insurance coverage documentation).

APRIL

- **April 1**
- Required Minimum Distributions (RMDs)** must begin if you turned **73 last year** and delayed your first RMD.
- **April 15 (or next business day if weekend/holiday)**
- **Personal Tax Filing Deadline (Form 1040)**
- **First Quarter Estimated Taxes Due**
- **Deadline to make prior-year contributions** to:
- Traditional IRA / Roth IRA
- SEP IRA
- HSA
- Coverdell Education Savings Account (ESA)
- **Last day to file for a 6-month tax extension** (Form 4868).
- **Last day to file FAFSA** in some states if applying for financial aid (for dependent children).

MAY

- **Early May**
- Review **property tax assessments** if applicable. Protest deadline usually mid-May depending on your state.
- **May 29 (5/29)**
- National **529 College Savings Plan Day** – Great reminder to review or open 529 accounts for children.

JUNE

- **June 15**
- **2nd Quarter Estimated Taxes Due**
- **U.S. Citizens Abroad** tax filing deadline (can extend to October 15).
- **Mid-June**
- Mid-year **retirement account performance review**. Adjust contributions if needed.
- Reassess **charitable giving** plans for the year.

JULY

- **July 1–15**
- **Mid-year financial check-in:**
- Review spending, savings goals, debt paydown progress.
- Rebalance portfolio if allocation is off by more than 5–10%.
- Schedule a **meeting with your financial advisor or CPA**.

AUGUST

- **August 1–31**
- Plan for **open enrollment** (usually starts in October or November).
- Review HSA/FSA balances and projected usage.
- **Review insurance policies**: life, disability, malpractice, and umbrella

coverage.

- Prep for **year-end charitable planning** (DAFs, appreciated stock, QCDs if age 70½+).

SEPTEMBER

- **September 15**
- **3rd Quarter Estimated Taxes Due**
- **Tax Deadline for Calendar-Year Partnerships and S-Corps (if on extension)**
- **Late September**
- Check for any **backdoor Roth IRA contributions** to convert before year-end.
- Consider **harvesting capital losses** to offset gains before Q4 ends.

OCTOBER

- **October 1**
- Deadline for **establishing a SIMPLE IRA** for current tax year.
- Medicare Open Enrollment preview window begins (important for you, parents, or retired patients).
- **October 15**
- **Extended Individual Tax Return Due Date** (Form 1040 with extension).
- **Deadline to fund SEP IRA** for prior year (if filed extension).
- **Deadline to recharacterize prior-year Roth IRA contributions**.
- **Late October**
- Review open enrollment options for employer-sponsored insurance.

NOVEMBER

- **November 1–30**
- **Health Insurance Open Enrollment** begins for ACA Marketplace.
- Employer benefits enrollment usually begins. Reassess:
- Health plans (HSA-eligible?)
- Life & disability insurance
- 401(k) contribution changes
- FSA/HSA elections
- Legal services or supplemental benefits
- **Black Friday Weekend**
- Consider timing large purchases with end-of-year spending and cash flow planning.

DECEMBER

- **December 1–15**
- **Last call to max out retirement accounts**:
- 401(k), 403(b), 457 contributions
- HSA contributions (if payroll deductions)
- Backdoor Roth conversion
- **December 31**
- **Last day for:**
- Charitable contributions to count for current year (check DAF cutoffs).
- **Tax-loss harvesting** (sell losers to offset capital gains).
- **RMDs for age 73+** (Required Minimum Distributions).
- **Gifting up to $18,000 per recipient** (annual exclusion for gift tax).
- Spend down **FSA funds** (check for grace period or carryover).
- Convert to Roth IRA (backdoor Roth deadline).
- Complete **year-end bonuses and profit-sharing contributions** for S-corps.

BONUS: Rolling & Event-Based Reminders

- **Every Paycheck:**
- Check 401(k)/403(b) deductions.
- Verify health/dental/vision premiums and HSA contributions.
- **After Major Life Events:**
- Marriage/divorce
- Birth/adoption of child
- New job or contract
- Disability or injury
- Change of primary residence
- Significant windfall/inheritance
- **Quarterly:**
- Revisit budget and spending.
- Make estimated tax payments if self-employed or have side income.
- Review investment performance and allocations.
- Meet with advisor if pursuing tax-loss harvesting or Roth conversions.

Final Tip: Automate What You Can

Set calendar reminders. Automate contributions. Set up recurring transfers. The less reliant you are on memory, the more consistent your wealth-building habits will become.

About the Author

Patrick Brown, MBA is a former Division I athlete turned financial advisor, educator, and advocate for financial literacy across professional industries. With over two decades of experience in wealth management, retirement planning, and insurance strategy, Patrick has worked with a wide range of high-performing professionals—including physicians, coaches, business owners, and attorneys.

Drawing from his own journey of learning about money the hard way, Patrick founded a suite of platforms dedicated to financial education, including:

- *Financial Literacy For NIL*
- *Financial Literacy For Student Athletes*
- *Financial Literacy For Doctors*
- *Financial Literacy For College Coaches*
- *Financial Literacy For The Culture*
- Parents Of Student Athletes

Through these initiatives, Patrick has become a trusted resource for professionals seeking real-world financial guidance tailored to their careers, lifestyles, and long-term goals.

In *Financial Literacy For Attorneys,* Patrick brings his proven framework to the legal field—guiding lawyers through every financial milestone, from law school to senior partner, and all the transitions in between. His writing is grounded in practical tools, relatable insights, and a deep respect for the complexity of the legal profession.

Whether you're a newly licensed associate managing student loans, a mid-career attorney navigating partnership decisions, or a seasoned professional planning for retirement and legacy—this book was written for you.

When he's not coaching clients or writing, Patrick serves as a hospital trustee, speaks at universities, and mentors young professionals on how to turn income into lasting impact. He lives with his wife and two daughters and continues to pursue his mission: to make financial literacy accessible, empowering, and actionable—for everyone.

Glossary of Financial Terms

1. Asset Allocation

The process of dividing investments among different asset classes (e.g., stocks, bonds, real estate) to balance risk and reward.

2. Capital Gains

Profit from the sale of an asset, such as stocks or real estate. Long-term capital gains (held over a year) are taxed at lower rates than short-term gains.

3. Compound Interest

Interest calculated on the original principal and also on the accumulated interest from previous periods. This helps investments grow exponentially over time.

4. Diversification

A risk management strategy that mixes a wide variety of investments within a portfolio to reduce exposure to any one asset or risk.

5. Emergency Fund

A cash reserve set aside to cover unexpected expenses or financial emergencies, typically 3–6 months of living expenses.

6. ETF (Exchange-Traded Fund)

A type of investment fund that is traded on stock exchanges, typically tracking an index, commodity, or sector.

7. Fiduciary

A person or organization legally bound to act in another party's best interest, such as a fiduciary financial advisor.

8. HSA (Health Savings Account)

A tax-advantaged savings account available with high-deductible health plans, used to pay for qualified medical expenses.

9. IRA (Individual Retirement Account)

A retirement account with tax benefits. Traditional IRAs allow pre-tax contributions; Roth IRAs are funded with after-tax dollars but offer tax-free withdrawals.

10. Liquidity

The ease with which an asset can be converted into cash without significantly affecting its value.

11. Net Worth

Your total assets minus total liabilities. A key measure of overall financial health.

12. Passive Income

Earnings derived from investments or business ventures in which the earner is not actively involved (e.g., rental income, dividends).

13. Portfolio

A collection of financial assets like stocks, bonds, mutual funds, and real estate owned by an individual or institution.

14. Rebalancing

The process of realigning the weightings of a portfolio's assets to maintain a desired risk level or asset allocation.

15. Risk Tolerance

An investor's ability and willingness to endure market volatility and potential loss of capital.

16. Roth Conversion

Transferring money from a Traditional IRA to a Roth IRA, triggering taxes now in exchange for tax-free growth and withdrawals later.

17. SEP IRA

A retirement plan for self-employed individuals and small business owners that allows higher contribution limits than traditional IRAs.

18. Solo 401(k)

A retirement savings plan for self-employed individuals, with both employee and employer contribution options.

19. Tax-Loss Harvesting

Selling losing investments to offset capital gains tax on winners, lowering overall tax liability.

20. Term Life Insurance

A life insurance policy that provides coverage for a specific period (e.g., 20 years) and pays a death benefit if the insured dies during the term.

21. Umbrella Insurance

A type of liability insurance that provides extra coverage beyond your auto and home insurance policies.

22. Vesting

The process by which an employee gains ownership of employer-contributed funds (e.g., in a 401(k)) over time.

23. Whole Life Insurance

A permanent life insurance policy that builds cash value and provides lifetime coverage—typically more expensive than term insurance.

24. Estate Planning

The process of arranging for the management and disposal of a person's estate during life and after death, often through wills, trusts, and powers of attorney.

25. RMD (Required Minimum Distribution)

The minimum amount that must be withdrawn annually from retirement accounts (like Traditional IRAs or 401(k)s) once the account holder reaches a certain age.

26. 529 Plan

A tax-advantaged savings plan designed to encourage saving for future education costs. Earnings grow tax-free when used for qualified expenses.

27. Credit Score

A number between 300 and 850 that represents a person's creditworthiness. Based on credit history, payment habits, and debt levels.

28. Budget

A financial plan for managing income and expenses over a specific period, used to avoid overspending and build savings.

29. Inflation

The rate at which the general level of prices for goods and services rises, reducing purchasing power over time.

30. Annuity

A financial product sold by insurance companies that provides regular payments, often used for retirement income.

Conclusion: Advocate for Yourself Like You Do for Others

Because Your Greatest Case Is the One You Make for Your Own Life

You've spent your career advocating for others.

You've stood beside clients in courtrooms, across conference tables, and behind closed doors. You've helped them navigate the fine print, fight for fairness, and make sense of chaos. You've spent late nights researching statutes, crafting arguments, and guiding people through some of the hardest moments of their lives.

But now it's your turn.

It's time to bring that same clarity, compassion, and courage to your **own financial life**.

Because for too long, even the most brilliant attorneys have lacked access to practical, trustworthy financial education. It's not taught in law school. It's not explained during onboarding at firms. And by the time you're earning six—or seven—figures, it often feels too late (or too awkward) to ask the questions you never got to ask.

This book has been about closing that gap.

It's not about mastering every nuance of taxes, trusts, or investment strategy. It's about **reclaiming ownership** over the decisions that shape your future. Whether you're fresh out of law school or a managing partner approaching retirement, financial literacy gives you three things every attorney needs:

- **Clarity**: Knowing where you stand, where you're headed, and what actions will move you forward

- **Confidence**: Feeling secure enough to make decisions—or ask for help when you need it
- **Control**: Building a life and career on your own terms, not one dictated by debt, fear, or uncertainty

This Isn't the End—It's the Start of Your Financial Next Chapter

You don't need to do everything at once. But you do need to do something. Here are some next steps you can take today:

- Schedule a financial review with your spouse, advisor, or even just yourself
- Set up automatic savings or increase your retirement contributions by 1%
- Draft or revisit your will, trust, and power of attorney documents
- Begin teaching your kids or mentees about budgeting and investing
- Make your first charitable gift—or formalize your giving strategy
- Review your insurance coverage, update beneficiaries, or consolidate old accounts
- Ask your firm's HR department to explain your benefits in detail

Your financial life isn't a separate project—it's the foundation for every other part of your life. When it's strong, you can focus more clearly on your practice, your family, and your purpose.

Lead by Example—For the Next Generation of Lawyers

By becoming more financially literate, you don't just help yourself—you help the entire legal community. You become the colleague who shares a useful resource. The partner who mentors younger associates. The parent who raises financially savvy kids. The friend who normalizes smart financial conversations.

You also become a better advocate for your clients—especially when they face their own money-related legal decisions.

Financial wellness isn't just about freedom—it's about *functioning at your best*.

Final Thoughts

Let this be your reminder: **you are your most important client**.

Advocate for yourself. Protect your time, your peace, and your future. Put yourself in the strongest position possible—not just in your career, but in your life.

You've got the tools now. The next move is yours.

And trust me—there's no one better for the job.

Made in United States
Orlando, FL
04 November 2026

90201064R00177